*One of four volumes covering four centuries
of Scottish interior decoration*

Renaissance Scotland was characterised by change. New prosperity as well as new learning brought forward a class of lairds and merchants who built rural and urban tower houses throughout Scotland, by the hundreds. These were homes in which domestic considerations gradually superseded the defensive function, but which retained a vertical, fortified form.

This was a time, too — between 1560 and the end of the 17th century — when, in the wake of the Protestant Reformation, alliances were formed or revitalised not only with England but also with the Scandinavian countries and the vibrant young Dutch republic whose cultural influence in Scotland is to be seen in everything from painted ceilings to published maps.

But the local manifestation of these influences was uniquely Scottish. The evocative tower houses have no parallel elsewhere in Europe. Built by local craftsmen, their interiors were finished with painted ceilings, painted walls, carved panelling and, later, finely decorated plasterwork.

But, by the 20th century, many tower house which had been handed down from generation to generation had fallen into disrepair or ruin.

In the last twenty years the rush to restore began in earnest. The purchasers of Towie Barclay and Peffermill House were only two of many families who saw the advantages in near-perfect internal layout: small, sensible roofs which would not cost the earth to maintain; walls eight feet thick to help keep in warmth; a good-sized living area in the Great Hall (complete with window recesses or 'sitooteries') and smaller family rooms off and on the third storey. And, over and above all other considerations, the fine, romantic adventure of making a castle their home.

We are grateful to the owners whose houses are featured in SCOTTISH RENAISSANCE INTERIORS. Within the framework of classic tower house form, readers will observe different approaches and styles — some have furnished lavishly, others simply; some have installed new painted ceilings, others have left them undecorated. And at least one owner is building his own tower house, from scratch.

None have adopted the popular misconception — that the interiors of Scottish houses four centuries ago were dour and bare. The painted ceilings which still exist in great numbers throughout Scotland are just one reminder of the colourful decorative expression favoured at the time. Rugs, tapestries, embroidered hangings, pottery, decorative metalwork, carved furniture and panelling are other elements in the beguiling interiors of the renaissance which married colour and freshness with simple forms and designs.

CONTENTS

SCOTTISH RENAISSANCE INTERIORS

MOUBRAY HOUSE PRESS
in association with
The National Trust for Scotland
and
Historic Houses Association for Scotland
ISBN 0 948473 06 1

Editor — Sheila Mackay
Series Consultants — John Gifford: Ian Gow
Sub-editor — Jeremy Bruce-Watt

Publisher — Nic Allen
Design — Dorothy Steedman at Graphic Partners
Photography — Douglas MacGregor

Advertising Associate — Margaret Wilson
Classified Advertising — Margaret Clezy
Advertising Design — Ros King

Administrative Assistant — Anne Whitaker

MOUBRAY HOUSE PRESS, 9/2 Tweeddale Court, 14 High Street, Edinburgh EH1 1TE.
Tel: 031-557 3349. Editorial Office, 53 High Street, Edinburgh EH1 1SR. Tel: 031-556 4402.

Typesetting by Anagram Word Services, Edinburgh. Colour separations by Marshall Thompson, Edinburgh. Printed by John Bartholomew & Son, Edinburgh.

Moubray House Press wishes to thank the owners of the houses featured in SCOTTISH RENAISSANCE INTERIORS: Marc and Karen Ellington, the Earl and Countess of Glasgow, Angus Grossart, Nicholas and Limma Groves-Raines, Schomberg Scott and The National Trust for Scotland. Thanks are also due to Ian Begg, Rosalind Marshall and Lennox Savage.

All photography by Douglas MacGregor except pp.5, 11, (James Crumley), pp.7, 8, 9, (Ian Begg), p.17, (Dave Paterson), pp.60-66, 83, (National Trust for Scotland). Photography of Towie Barclay and Cullen House ceilings by Eric Ellington.

The following photographs are reproduced by kind permission of Peter Maxwell-Stuart p.12, Glasgow Museums and Galleries pp.13, 15, Conservation Bureau, SDA p.17, Christies p.68, National Galleries of Scotland p.72, Marquess of Lothian p.73, National Museums of Scotland p.74

Front cover: Moubray House consists of two houses. The vaulted room is in the upper house, referred to as the 'heich hoose' in a 16th century title deed. George Jamesone, Scotland's first portrait painter, lived in Moubray House in the 17th century.

Back cover: Corner of the Great Hall, Peffermill House.

SMALLBONE
HAND PAINTED KITCHENS

On a Venetian theme: aquamarine softly washed over broken cream with outlined faux-marbling. The coolness of the flagstones is contrasted with the richness of the fabric and hand-painted tiles.

At our beautiful showroom in the heart of Edinburgh you can experience the special atmosphere of genuine Smallbone kitchens and bedrooms. We have proved ourselves the leading designers, manufacturers and fitters of hand crafted, fitted kitchens and bedrooms. Choose from Old Pine, Oak or Hand-painted Kitchens and Chestnut and Hand-painted Bedrooms. A Smallbone designer can come to your home and create an individual design based on our unique concept.

26 CASTLE ST. EDINBURGH 031 225 8222

SCI/0006/87K

TOWERING ASPIRATION

A career spent rescuing some of Scotland's finest tower houses from forlorn decrepitude has inspired architect Ian Begg to build his own — Ravens' Craig in Wester Ross. *James Crumley* visited the building site of this 'post-modernist-neo-baronial broch'

It is a familiar enough scene in the Scottish Highlands, the ragged shell of half a roofless wall peering fearfully for foes over the advancing green-bannered armies of one more spring's birches. One more hasty glance across a hillside in Wester Ross might conclude that this is one more gaunt monument to one more long-gone laird's territorial ambition, struggling even now to repel the trees' advance, a monument whose commandments and comments are told in tablets of old stone or whispered by winds and weeds.

Look again. On the Loch Carron shore near Plockton, the road curving up through the birches is no weedy hangover, no ghost's thoroughfare. It is newly cut and its fringing geans have been hand-planted this spring. The shell when you reach it is a building site, full of the stushie and stour of creativity. These walls are rising, not crumbling, and their unique story is told not in tablets of stone but in blocks of concrete.

As for the laird's territorial ambitions, these are almost disappointingly modest — they harbour no greater aggression than planting oaks for posterity round some of his marches to counter the worst excesses of his Chelsea neighbour's long-distance predilection for under-planting the resident birches with Sitka spruce.

Ian Begg, architect, Fife-born, Edinburgh-based, Wester-Ross-inclined, has taken his life's work thus far to a logical conclusion of a kind. The man whose architectural pedigree was fashioned by a trilogy of benevolent forces — homage to Charles Rennie Mackintosh, the guiding hand of the architect Robert Hurd, and an instinctive gut reaction of warmth for the Scottish tradition — is building his own tower house. In concrete.

The building's design and materials are governed by that distillation of hard-

5

Mappin Plate – the finest plated silver in the world.
Above: Octagonal Tea Service, also in Sterling Silver.
Catalogue available upon request.

Mappin & Webb

LONDON · PARIS · DUSSELDORF

88 George Street Edinburgh Tel: 031-225 5502 · 67 Vincent Street Glasgow Tel: 041-221 7683 · Gleneagles Hotel Auchterarder Perthshire Tel: 07646 3383
170 Regent Street London W1 Tel: 01-734 3801 · 65 Brompton Road Knightsbridge London SW3 Tel: 01-584 9361

headed practicality, flourished ingenuity and reverential respect for tradition which imbue the character of the architect. The fact of the building is the unabashed romantic in the man, which none of these other qualities and commodities has ever quite held in check.

He would love to have built in stone of course — who wouldn't with a track record which boasts of some of the most accomplished modern restorations of tower houses and other historic architectural treasures in the land? Cost precluded stone, and besides, the use of concrete permits Ian Begg to practise persuasively what he preaches, which is the value of the Scottish tradition as a force with an architectural future.

The tower house tradition, in as far as it had evolved by the renaissance

Beldorney 'turned out to be much older than its owners thought'

years, has been allowed to dictate the principles of design. Thus the lowest ground floor level which the hillside affords is a basement and it is the door on the hill side of the house which opens directly into the prerequisite architectural feature, the vaulted room.

The place is a beguilement of arches. The first of these is the principal entrance of the inner wall — a double wall, with stairs and nooks and chambers and crannies between, is a feature of the tower house established 2000 years ago in the brochs. It is when you consider the broch as the blueprint from which the tower house evolved that you finally grasp the appeal of this project to its instigator. The broch was both uniquely Scottish, and an architectural phenomenon — qualities which anyone who has enjoyed so much as a five minute conversation with Ian Begg would recognise as endearing to him.

His sentiments have substantial support in Stewart Cruden's book *The Scottish Castle*. 'The origin of the style,' writes Cruden, 'is wholly constructional, and the style so arresting as to imply a preconceived notion. It was an idea before it was a fact — the idea of a highly original mind . . . It is the most remarkable ancient castle in Europe.'

But back to arches. Ian Begg's vaulted room in his post-modernist-neo-baronial-broch is already instinctively atmospheric, even in its raw unplastered rubble-strewn state. Other arches reach through the double wall to deeply recessed windows, others to stairs modest and grand, one to a quiet contemplative corner. Pursue another and a lift shaft emerges. The lift may never be fitted, but the architect has provided for it just in case . . . well, perhaps just in case his easy way with the stairs of three-and-a-half stories dwindles with the years.

The vaulted ceiling dominates that place of arches — it too is of traditionally laid concrete blocks — and in the half light which prevails there, even in a sunlit noon, it already hints at antiquity, which is to compliment its architect and the rare virtuosity of a Plockton mason called Roddy McKenzie.

The principal staircase climbs a turret in a broad spiral to the Great Hall, and for all the tradition in the later tower houses of bold, even lurid, painted ceilings, it was a unique moment to climb the staircase and emerge into the still roofless Hall with the wide horizons of Loch Carron and the Applecross hills for a ceiling. It is some time since anyone in Scotland saw a roofless Great Hall before the roof was built as opposed to after it had collapsed.

The design for the Hall's ceiling underlines the romantic — even the whimsical — in the nature of the architect. Small triangular panels in red and green each bear a motif which reflects some aspect, some old throwback, some souvenir, some of life's milestones for the tower's resident family. The artist is Norman Edgar from the Clyde coast. By contrast, the floor of the Hall is a more sombre affair of square stone tiles set in a timber grid.

This, you sense, will be the most gleeful of the many satisfactions which Ian Begg derives from the project — the deliberate stamping of

Top and middle: Muckrach, before and after restoration;
Above left: Tillycairn;
Above Right: Aboyne. All projects in which Ian Begg

personality onto the fabric of the building in the manner which is the unique prerogative of the laird who is also the architect.

A third floor houses bedrooms, and features a projecting timber bartizan.

was involved during his tower house restoring days with Robert Hurd and Partners

That, in the architect's phrase 'should be a pretty impressive place' — a spectacular tower-top eyrie for steady heads who like their horizons wide. Above that — a slate-capped attic.

One experimental innovation is a floor-warming system for heating the vaulted room and to a lesser and unpredictable extent the Hall, using the spaces on either side of the vault to house two long cylindrical hot water tanks. A pump takes the water into the floor of the vaulted room and the presence of the tanks themselves will provide some warmth for the Hall.

Another innovation harks back rather than forward. The prospect of internal phones to solve the practical problem of communication between floors did not appeal. Speaking tubes did. Roddy McKenzie has accommodated these with the same philosophical shrug with which he confronts any unlikely commission. Ian Begg was well enough known in the area before the tower house — his more conventional Highland home is a quarter of a mile away on the same hillside — so that a wry humour permeates the building site banter. Ian's insistence on natural 'unfinished' finishes prompted an instruction from Roddy to ensure that there was a bit of peat mixed in with each batch of cement 'because Mr Begg wants to encourage moss to grow on the walls'. That kind of thing.

The tower house Ian Begg calls Ravens' Craig is a repository for the ideas, gleanings, instincts and all the other less specific by-products of an architectural career which chose to steep itself in the riches on its own doorstep. At the back of his mind when he designed his new home — colouring his thinking rather than dictating it — was Muckrach, a 16th century tower house near Dulnain Bridge in Strathspey which he restored from forlorn decrepitude to former glories.

Other distinguished restorations have included Rossend Castle at

With the establishment of our new workrooms, Shapes now offer a complete interior furnishing service for carpets, wall coverings, loose covers and curtains.

The new ranges of soft upholstery include Parker & Farr which complement our extensive range of international fabrics, all of which can be seen in our showrooms at Colinton.

Largest display of quality reproduction furniture in Scotland.
Over 3000 pieces on display or in stock.

Leasing Facilities for all Business Furniture

Showroom, 6 West Mill Road, (off Woodhall Road) Colinton, Edinburgh 031 441 7963 Open 7 days 9—5 p.m. Sunday 12—5 p.m.

All retail and office or hotel contract enquiries welcome. Export orders taken for worldwide distribution. Custom built furniture for the discerning.

Burntisland in Fife as offices for Robert Hurd and Partners, and Beldorney in the Deveron Valley near Huntly, both when he was a partner in the firm. Beldorney was significant 'because we were able to demonstrate for very good reasons that it was older than its owners had thought'. A vault had been inserted in an earlier building as the tower house was built.

Ian Begg was also brought in to do major restoration work at Blair Castle where a Clayton ceiling had fallen in. 'We put that back,' he explains, as though it was that simple. There is also the little local difficulty of re-covering all that formidable castle's external walls. The original lime had been coated with emulsion paint, reducing its resistance to all manner of meteorological hells. By comparison with under-takings like these, building

from the drawing board — even building a tower house — can seem remarkably and refreshingly simple.

It is a short stride from Plockton over a ferry and a headland or two to the broch of Dun Fiadhairt on the Isle of Skye. I was there — I have been there many times over many years — two weeks after visiting Ian Begg at Loch Carron. With the terns screaming over Garbh Eilein, the seals sclaffing the placid waters of Dunvegan Loch and herons silhouetted against the sunset at Camalag Bay, I saw this old rickle of stones in a new perspective. There are few enough of us who could chart a passage from the brochs to breeze blocks and make it sound logical. Ian Begg is one of the few.

The site of Ravens' Craig on the shore of Loch Carron

EMBROIDERED BED

Renaissance four-posters were on view for all to see, in palaces and humble homes alike. Curtains were a necessity for privacy as well as warmth, and *Margaret Swain* has discoverd that even Mary, Queen of Scots, took up her needle to decorate hangings

Until the 18th century the bed was probably the most public and often the most expensive item of furniture in a large house. Children slept on truckle beds, servants on pallets, but the imposing four-posted bed in the chief bedroom was the stage upon which the drama of life and death took place. It was there that the mother, newly delivered from the perils of childbirth, received the congratulations of visitors come to see the new infant; where sorrowing relatives took leave of the dying, and where the corpse was laid out before the burial. We, who now accept the anonymity of the hospital bed for our beginning and our end, find such publicity in what has now become a private room, distasteful. Our ancestors were more robust in their approach to reality.

The four-posted bed, with enclosing curtains, tester and narrow flat upper valance ('pand' in Scottish inventories) that hid the curtain rods, remained remarkably unchanged from medieval times to the end of the 17th century, when the ornate baroque bed, with its richly fringed draperies and elaborate tester, became the fashion. The stand, or frame of the bed, was secondary to its textile hangings. Indeed, in inventories, a 'Bed', or 'Bed furniture' referred to such hangings. The stand is rarely specified,

Opposite: part of an embroidered panel showing borage, tulip and other flowers. One of several panels for decorative hangings discovered recently at Traquair House, uncut and unused, still showing the brilliant colours chosen to decorate bedhangings in the late 16th and early 17th century; Above: Hans Memling (c1430-94) showed the Virgin's bed hung with red curtains (one looped up) with a narrow flat pelmet that hides the curtain rods in his painting of the Annunciation, now in the Burrell Collection. The tester is probably suspended from the ceiling, and not held up by posts at the corners, but the shape of the bed remained remarkably constant from medieval times until the end of the 17th century

Are you looking for a traditional or modern bed skilfully crafted in solid wood? Matching bedroom furniture and beautiful bedlinens in every design, style and colour?
And So To Bed is the only bedroom specialist where you can find the best of everything under one roof.
The finest quality and craftsmanship is the hallmark of our success. New models are constantly being added to our ranges. Come and take a look for yourself and you'll see why we're known as

And·So·To·Bed

The 'complete bedroom shop'

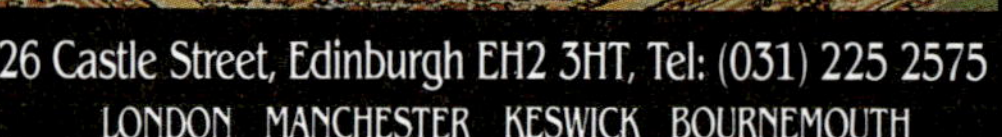

For colour catalogues, please write or phone to our showroom. 26 Castle Street, Edinburgh EH2 3HT, Tel: (031) 225 2575
LONDON MANCHESTER KESWICK BOURNEMOUTH

Valance from a bed, once at Balloch (Taymouth Castle), now in the Burrell Collection. The Campbell and Ruthven arms are surmounted by the initials of Sir Colin Campbell of Glenorchy and his wife, Katherine Ruthven, whom he married in 1550. The embroidered panels would have been mounted onto velvet or silk

since it was completely hidden. It was of pine, 'firr wood', which is susceptible to woodworm and therefore did not last as long as the hangings. The mattresses, for there were at least two, one filled with straw, the other a feather mattress, valued for its weight of feathers, rested on a 'canvas bottom'. This was a rectangle of sailcloth, with reinforced eyelets through which ropes were threaded, lashing the canvas to the beams at the side, head and foot of the bed. The imposing red damask bed at Blair Castle, in the Tapestry Room, still retains its canvas bottom. A 'lath bottom': battens of wood to support the mattress, gradually became more acceptable.

The surrounding curtains were a necessity, not only for warmth, but also for privacy, when room opened into room. Woollen cloth was usual: at Balloch, now Taymouth Castle, red 'London cloth' and 'green London cloth' beds were listed in 1640. In Edinburgh 'striped Musselburgh cloth', a coarse woollen, was used. For the more ostentatious, velvet or even silk was chosen, with embroidered designs on the pelmet and on the curtains as well The inventories of Mary, Queen of Scots, and her mother, Mary of Guise, indicate what could be seen in the royal palaces:

A bed of broderie work on four colours of satin, red, blue, yellow and white.

A bed of crimson velvet embroidered with phoenixes and tears (the emblem of Mary of Guise).

A bed of black velvet embroidered with arms and spheres.

Another of brown velvet with applied gold and silver, with ciphers and flowers embroiderd in silk and gold.

Another with true lovers' knots and the Greek letters . . . (for Francis II of France, the first husband of Mary Queen of Scots).

Yet another had the Labours of Hercules embroidered on it. This was later repaired for the visit to Scotland in 1619 of Mary's son, James VI and I, and was afterwards taken to Hampton Court, where it remained till the Commonwealth.

During Mary's years in Scotland, from 1561 to 1568, her upholsterers and her embroiderers laboured to repair bed hangings and to make new ones, some given as wedding gifts to her ladies.

Such splendour and invention were reflected in the larger houses of Scotland. A set of three valances that decorated the bed of Sir Colin Campbell of Glenorchy and his wife Katherine Ruthven, whom he married in 1550, are now well displayed in the Burrell Collection. Sir Colin died

in 1585, and as she was a second wife it may be assumed that they were made soon after the marriage.

They are embroidered in silk and wool, and all three display the Campbell arms. The shortest, for the foot of the bed, shows them impaling the Ruthven arms with a true lovers' knot suspended from a ram's head, the Ruthven supporter. On either side is a lively representation of the Temptation of Adam and Eve, and their expulsion from Paradise: an unlikely design for a couple who had four sons and four daughters.

A number of narrow valances in tent stitch on canvas survives from Scottish castles in the Perthshire area — some with well-drawn figures depicting biblical or mythological scenes, wearing French costume fashionable at the time of Mary, Queen of Scots, or slightly later. Inevitably, some have been attributed to her needle, though the drawing and execution suggest a professional workshop. Certainly she worked panels for hangings. William Drummond of Hawthornden described an elaborate set of bedhangings made by her, embellished with embroidered emblems. The bed has disappeared. Her surviving embroidery, worked while she was a prisoner in England during the last part of her life, has indeed been mounted on to hangings of green velvet. They are small panels of canvas work, octagonal or cruciform in shape, worked in cross stitch in silk. Many of them, signed with her initials or cipher, have personal associations, like the leaping dolphin — a visual pun, for her first husband was Le Dauphin when she married him. The French word can mean either the fish or the eldest son of the king.

Small panels like this were easy to work, since they only required a small frame that could be carried around. They were an economical way of decorating a large area. Single motifs of flowers, animals and insects were worked on canvas, then stiffened on the back before being cut out and applied to hangings of velvet or silk: indeed, they could be re-mounted on to new material when the old wore out, as curtains were apt to do. A bed decorated in this way, in use till the last war, can be seen at Scone Palace, its original red velvet now faded to a tawny hue. Scores of such flower motifs, intended to decorate hangings, survive at Traquair House, uncut and unused, their bright colours unfaded. They remind us how needlework provided colour and decoration for interiors that we now mistakenly imagine were cold and bare.

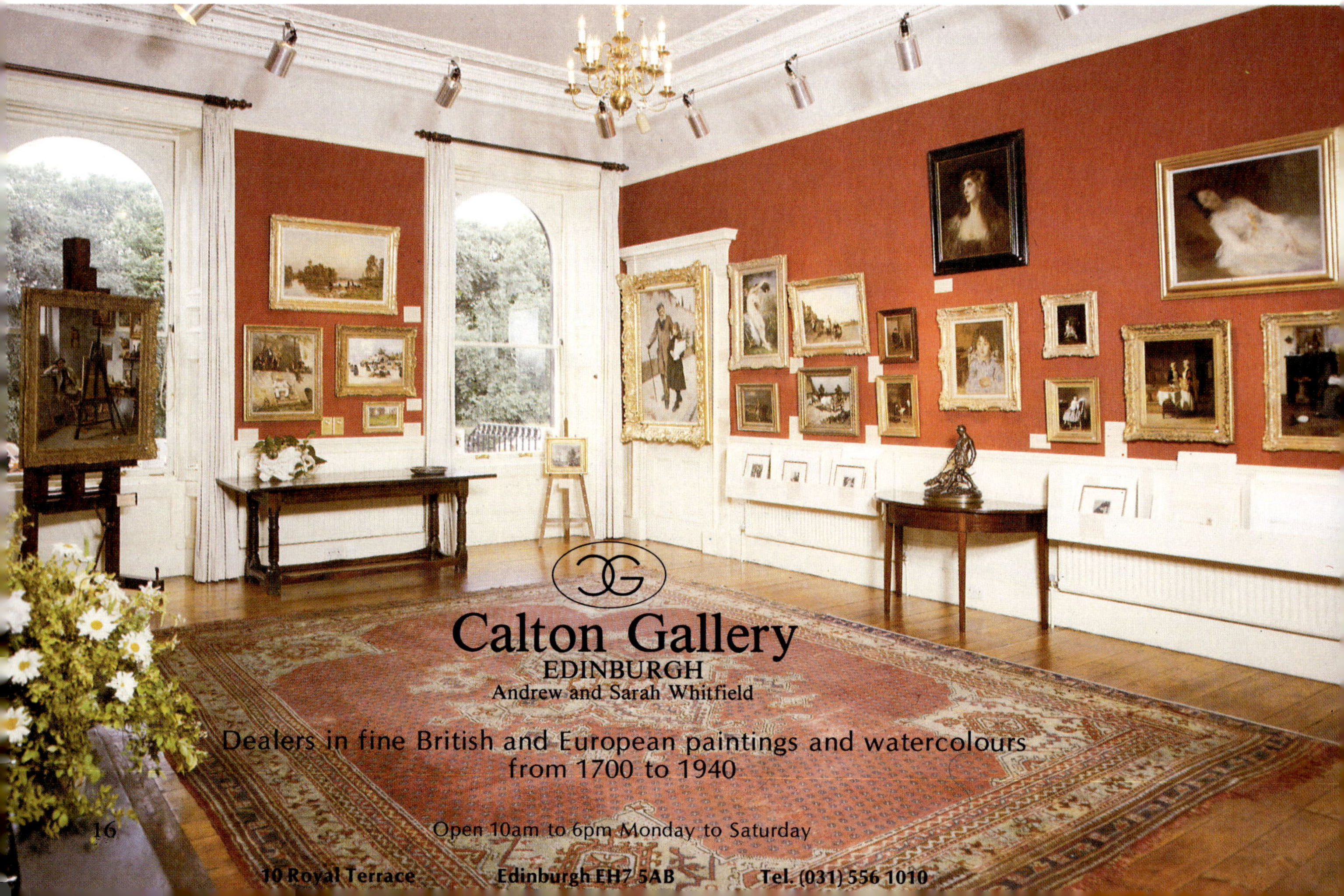

ARTFUL CRAFT

Post-reformation Scots liked their ceilings painted in a riot of colours and designs. As *Nic Allen* observes, many still survive and are painstakingly preserved by Stenhouse Conservation Centre

John Currie of Stenhouse Conservation Centre at work on the painted ceiling of St. Mary's, Grandtully, an unusual example of a ceiling painted in a church after the Reformation

If you had walked into the home of any prosperous Scottish merchant three hundred years ago, the chances are that you would have looked up to wooden ceilings covered with figurative or natural motifs and patterns, all emblazoned in a riot of blues, blacks, reds, ochres, greens and yellows. This was a particularly Scottish phenomenon: domestic painted ceilings of the late 16th and early 17th centuries appear to be as rare in England as they were common in Scotland.

Why was this so? Perhaps the most important factor was Lowland Scotland's shortage of accessible timber for building. By the 16th century this shortage was being made good by the import of Scandinavian and Baltic softwoods. These were adequate enough for building purposes but hardly had the aesthetic quality of English hardwoods. They needed covering and (in the absence of any extensive ornamental plasterwork tradition in Scotland until the mid-

17th century) the answer was to import the Continental penchant for ceiling painting along with the wood itself.

That explanation fits in well with the chronology of Scottish ceiling paintings, the first dated example of which is Prestongrange, East Lothian (1581) and the last the Skelmorlie Aisle, Largs (1638). There are likely to have been a number of undated ceilings painted outside these dates but it is clear that once ornamental plasterwork became available it directly superseded painted decoration. An interesting example of this evolution is to be seen at Moubray House in Edinburgh's High Street, where the grand second floor room was given an ornate plasterwork in the 1670s leaving the humbler top floor to exhibit traces of ceiling painting dated 1600 on its barrel vaulted ceiling.

Despite the Continental influences, the artists who actually undertook the work of painting ceilings were, almost without exception, Scots. Stylistic similarities would suggest that a single artist or group of artists worked over a wide area. There are, for instance, such similarities in ceilings as far apart as Culross and Burntisland in Fife and Cullen House in Banffshire which appear to indicate they might be the work of the same hand. Artists included family groups such as the Binnings and Workmans of Edinburgh who passed their skills from father to son throughout the latter part of the 16th century.

Painted decoration was applied to two types of ceiling. Firstly, and most commonly, there were the simple open-beam-and-board ceilings of the kind which survive at Northfield and Crathes. Here the ceiling consisted simply of the supporting beams and floorboards of the room above. Secondly, there was the grander, more costly construction in which the timber was used to create covered, elliptical or barrel-vaulted ceilings within the roof space. A fine example was the coved ceiling at Cullen which, sadly, was destroyed in a fire in June 1987. Ceilings like this provided a surface area on which the artist could spread out his creation in a freer manner than was possible within the confines of a beam and board ceiling.

The subject matter of the decorations contains both Scottish and foreign influences. There were mythological and biblical figures as well as floral, fruit and animal motifs, often translated crudely but effectively by local artists from the recently introduced Continental tapestries or iconographic manuals like Conrad Gessner's *Animalicum* of 1551. There were also heraldic motifs and patterns with a distinctly Celtic feel to them like those reproduced on the ceiling at Huntingtower Castle, Perthshire.

Sometimes there was a mixture of symbolism. When the relatively modest shipowner's home in Burntisland, Fife, known as Mary Sommerville's House, was restored in 1957 fragments of painting were found depicting religious and mythological scenes as well as the zodiac. At Prestongrange, the painted ceiling discovered in 1962 includes several grotesque figures with exaggerated sexual organs. Those figures may have been taken from a series of French engravings. But they have also been associated with the practice of Black Magic. Prestongrange is only a short distance from North Berwick which gave its name to the infamous witch trials of the 1580s.

A similarly well-endowed figure is to be found on the ceiling of John Knox House in the High Street, Edinburgh. Its appearance in the supposed home of the great reformer was too much for the Free Church, which owned the building in the 19th century. It was cut out of the ceiling,

hidden in the basement, and only rediscovered and reinstated during recent restoration work.

These ceilings represent many other dramatic examples of a process of rediscovery which has taken place dozens of times in Scotland over the past thirty years. So often, in fact, that surface decoration in paint, in at least fragmented form, is almost certain to be found whenever later coverings are removed from Scottish domestic ceilings of the late 16th or early 17th centuries.

The maintenance of Scotland's painted ceilings is now largely in the hands of Stenhouse Conservation Centre, Edinburgh, which, by making a speciality of this particular work, straddles the fields of fine art and architectural conservation. Stenhouse is now part of the Scottish Development Department's Directorate of Historic Buildings and Monuments and regularly carries out conservation work on decorations in the Directorate's guardianship such as those on the magnificent barrel-vaulted ceilings of the grandiosely named Culross Palace, the home of George Bruce, Fife's premier merchant prince in the late 16th century.

However, the Centre was originally established by the National Trust for Scotland for which it is still undertaking painted ceiling conservation (at Crathes Castle, for instance, or Gladstone's Land, a merchant's house in Edinburgh's Lawnmarket) as well as for private clients.

It is painstaking work, but of a kind in which Stenhouse conservators take a particular delight because it reveals a peculiarly — not to say idiosyncratically — domestic art form. As Stenhouse's Principal Conservator, Rab Snowden, says, the decorated ceilings of Scotland may seem naive when set beside the contemporary art of Rubens and Rembrandt, but they provide a fascinating insight into the cultural and aesthetic needs of post-Reformation Scotland.

Gone but not forgotten: the restoration of the magnificent painted ceiling at Cullen House, with its images of Mercury and Flora against a celestial background, was one of the early projects undertaken by Stenhouse Conservation Centre. Tragically, the ceiling was destroyed by fire just as Scottish Renaissance Interiors *was going to press*

TOWIE BARCLAY

The pink-harled castle of Towie Barclay is just visible from the road north to Turriff in Aberdeenshire. *John Gifford* turned aside to investigate

When Marc and Karen Ellington bought Towie Barclay in 1969 the castle had long ceased to be the residence of a laird. In the late 18th century it housed a tenant farmer who removed its top two storeys, then it became a Free Church Sunday School and more recently an agricultural shed. The Ellingtons restored the surviving floors of the original building, added a tall caphouse within the Victorian parapet, and covered the rubble masonry with harling as a gentle contrast to the dressed stonework of windows and doors. Now, with the Scottish saltire flying from the battlements, the house again looks as though it might be the stronghold of a feudal baron.

For five centuries the lands of Towie were held by the Barclays who gave their name to the castle. Their ancestor John de Berkeley is said to have been an Anglo-Norman knight who accompanied Queen Margaret to Scotland on her marriage to Malcolm III and was granted estates in the northern kingdom. One of his sons, Sir Alexander Barclay, inherited Towie — a 16th century stone on the castle names him as first of the line of Barclays of Towie. Another stone records that his descendant Sir Walter Barclay 'foundet' the castle in 1210. A later Sir Walter received a Crown charter of the lands of 'Tolly' from Robert the Bruce, and succeeding generations of Barclays seem quite at home in Aberdeenshire intermarrying with such leading families of the North-east as the Inneses, Gordons, Hays and Forbeses. The male line of the Barclays ended in 1668 with the death of Patrick Barclay, whose estates passed to his daughter Elizabeth, wife of John Gordon of Rothiemay. In 1752 Towie Barclay was sold to the Earl of Findlater and two centuries of neglect began.

The first buildings at Towie were probably of wood set within a palisade which reinforced the natural defences of the site, but by 1559 there was a stone-built 'castell'. Some of its walls may be incorporated in the present house which was created by the 17th Barclay laird, Sir Patrick,

after he succeeded his father in 1587. Perhaps as a preliminary to expensive building work Sir Patrick sold his Perthshire estate of Kerkow the year after he inherited, but he may have underestimated the cost for in 1599 he sold another estate, Auld Bourtie, after placing above his new front door a stone which sadly relates that 'In tym of valth al men seemis frindly ane frind is not knavin but in adversitie.'

For building his house Sir Patrick seems to have used a master mason who had worked at the nearby Gight Castle, where the same swastika mason's mark appears, and perhaps also at Craig Castle and Delgaty. Sir Patrick's master mason provided a solid L-shaped tower, given a strongly defensive appearance by the wide-mouthed gunloops gaping through the ground floor walls, although the larger first floor windows hint at comfort inside.

Inside the front door Sir Patrick Barclay's ownership was made clear to the visitor — the thick ribs of the square vestibule's groin vault meet at a boss carved with his arms and initials. A tunnel-vaulted passage runs through the house, passing on its left the kitchen, now with an Aga stove in place of an open fire, and on the right the vaulted dining room converted from Sir Patrick's wine cellar. The passage ends in a straight flight of four steps where the Ellingtons have hung a 16th century suit of armour made in Nuremburg for the export market — Sir Patrick could have owned just such a suit of armour. Then a broad turnpike stair leads up to the Great Hall.

The Great Hall is a magnificent demonstration of baronial status, its Gothic character perhaps deliberately archaic to recall the long association of the Barclays with Towie. The entrance vestibule's groin vault is reproduced here, but now on a massive scale and covering two large bays. The ribs begin low down the walls, springing from corbels carved with human heads and foliage. At the north corners are a corbel carved with the Barclay arms and another with only a plain shield, probably intended to be painted with the arms of the reigning mistress of the house. The ribs meet at carved and painted bosses, their sides carved with snakes and dogs' heads, copied from Pictish stones in the neighbourhood. On the underside of one boss are the royal arms of Scotland, the unicorn supporters looking decidedly strange — perhaps the reason why the carver felt it necessary to add the words *Arma Regis* (the King's Arms). On the other boss are the impaled arms of Barclay and Lamont and the words 'Patrick Barclay Lamond' suggesting that Sir Patrick married a Lamont as his second wife (his first was Janet Elphinstone).

The huge fireplace is an inglenook with narrow stone benches along its sides. Above each bench is an aumbry framed by delicate carved Gothic stonework under a carved rose. Away from the warmth of the fire are more comfortable-looking stone seats in the embrasure of the east window, through which the owner could look out for guests coming to the front door. Stepping out of the embrasure he would look back to the hall's south wall, whose upper part opens through a broad arch into an oratory. On each side of the arch is a pinnacled image niche now covered by a wooden angel carved in southern Germany in the late 17th century.

On the oratory's ceiling the heraldic scheme of the hall bosses reaches its culmination. After the coats of arms of the King and Sir Patrick Barclay, here is the coat of arms of Christ Himself (the *Arma Christi*) with His pierced hands and feet surrounding His heart. Set into the oratory's east wall is a stone altar slab with, above it, a corbel carved with a skull and crossbones intended to support a small statue. Sir Patrick Barclay

was a Roman Catholic who in 1589 had signed the Band for Defence of the True Religion against Protestantism. In this oratory he could hear Mass, perhaps with his servants watching from the Great Hall below.

The Ellingtons have not attempted to furnish the Great Hall as a 'period room' but their collection of furniture and pictures richly complements the architecture. Among the portraits are James VI of Scotland and his wife Anne of Denmark, the Old and Young Pretenders, Montrose's enemy the Earl of Argyll, and Anne, Countess of Findlater, whose son bought Towie Barclay in 1752. Foreign royalty such as Edward VI of England and Ferdinand I of Spain strike a cosmopolitan note, which is reinforced by a number of Old Masters including a peasant scene by Pieter Breughel the younger and a *Noli Me Tangere* attributed to Lucas Cranach the elder, showing St Mary Magdalene wearing a very expensive 16th century dress in order to meet the risen Lord.

17th century Scottish chairs join with a solid Dutch table to provide a solidity against which an early 18th century French clock can provide a contrast of baroque exuberance. One piece which Sir Patrick Barclay might even have known is the court cupboard of 1613 placed in a window embrasure. This was made for Tilquhilly Castle near Banchory and now carries a collection of Scottish pewter including communion plate from a Secession chapel at Sanquhar. The chapel's rigorously Presbyterian worshippers might have been shocked to find their plate in the same room as a 15th century crucifix but perhaps no more so than would have been James VI, the author of *A Counterblaste to Tobacco*, had he known that his portrait would have to survey the scene through the present owner's pipe-smoke. But smoking in Towie Barclay must surely have been welcome after 1614, when Sir Patrick Barclay's brother William published *Nepenthes, or the Vertues of Tabacco*, in which he hailed the weed as 'the only medicament in the world ordained by nature to entertaine good companie.'

PEFFERMILL PERFECTED

In less than ten years, the 17th century house which had fallen victim to the 20th century has been transformed. *Fay Young* relates an inspiring before-and-after story

A battering ram of a telegraph pole had broken down the front door; the garden was full of burnt-out cars and washing machines and giant hogweed surrounded the house; inside, rain leaked through holes in the roof where the lead flashing had been stripped away; almost every bath, hand basin and lavatory pan was smashed. The fortified house, built to protect a 17th century laird and his wife, had succumbed to 20th century attack.

'God will provyd' said the stone inscription above the entrance which had survived the onslaught and underneath a family motto in Latin: 'While I live I hope, God gives to whom he wishes.'

The motto was right. Where others would have turned away Nicholas Groves-Raines and Kristin Hannesdotir stayed and saw potential for a family home with room for their architects' business in the L-shaped turreted house unsuccessfully boarded up against invasion. The result is a transformation to delight all lovers of a before-and-after story.

In place of giant hogweed grow honeysuckle, herbs and old-fashioned roses. The turnpike stair leads up to a Great Hall retrieved from the damage caused by Victorian partitions and plastering in the 1880s and the vandals of a century later. What seemed an outwardly dark

*Above: the spiral or turnpike staircase leading to the floor above the Great Hall (the somewhat grandiose name given nowadays to describe what was the communal area in tower houses). As at Peffermill, this spacious room, which derived from the Viking 'longhouse' or 'firehouse', always incorporated a large fireplace and hearth; **Opposite:** a corner of the Great Hall provides good light for reading or sewing. The floor boards are painted off-white as a simple background for colourful rugs. A wooden-framed mirror reflects the images of the daughters of the house with their dog*

and daunting house is un-expectedly full of light: a warm and comfortable family house with offices in the originally vaulted kitchens of the ground floor. Between the Jolly Giant toy superstore and Craigmillar Industrial Estate, a few minutes drive from Edinburgh city centre, there is an almost unseen pocket of a 17th century country estate now closer to its origins than it has been for over 100 years, and possibly more romantic than Sir Walter Scott's view of 1830.

'Exactly such as a child would build with cards,' was Scott's description of the house with the central stair tower and steep crow-stepped gable when he used it as the seat of the Laird of Dumbiedykes in *The Heart of Midlothian.* He saw it among one or two dilapidated outhouses and 'a gallant crop' of docks and thistles. 'The whole argued neglect and discomfort: the con-sequence, however, of idleness and indifference, not of poverty.'

A house of mixed fortunes, Peffermill House: from laird's house to 18th century school for the deaf (visited by Samuel Johnson) to 20th century rented accommodation finally used by the local authority as a council house. For most of its life it has been a leasehold property. Built in 1636 for Edward Edgar and Margaret Pearson whose family coat of arms is inscribed above the main door, Peffermill House was bought by Sir John Gilmour in 1661 as part of the Craigmillar Castle estate and until 1982 remained the property of the Gilmour of Liberton family trust.

By the time Kristin Hannes-dotir and Nick Groves-Raines saw it in 1980 the house had been empty for some time. Being architects, restorers of old properties, and parents of three children whose holidays are spent camping in the grounds of Grade A listed places undergoing renovation, they were undaunted by the 'neglect and discomfort' they saw.

It took lengthy negotiations to persuade the local authority to sell but by November 1980 they had bought the leasehold for £500 (subsequently acquiring the freehold for £5,000 more). A year and twenty-five skips of rubbish later it was transformed into a light and airy building with caretakers' flat on the second floor, architects' business in the old cellars and a family home in

*Opposite: the tranquil dining-area of the Great Hall, overlooks mature trees in the garden. The oak gate-leg table is 17th century, the Persian plate appropriate in its blue-and-white glaze; **Above:** the Great Hall is the drawing room of the house nowadays, its hearth still the focal point of the room. Pale emulsion paint covers the walls, but a strip of the original painted decoration, which would have covered large areas, survives behind the far door. A mixture of junk shop 'finds' and family heirlooms furnish the room in a pleasing variety of styles, unified by the simplicity of the loose covers on the chairs and sofa, and the painted floor-boards*

the rest of the house. 'Ideally,' says Kristin, (otherwise known as Limma), 'it should all be one house with the kitchen on the ground floor to make use of the enormous original fireplace — and a back door out to the formal herb and rose garden we are recreating.'

But one of the secrets of living in castles is to find a working compromise between the aesthetic demands of the past and the economic realities of the present. So their kitchen takes the place of an old bedroom off the Great Hall: Victorian sash windows let in more light than the original half-shuttered lead lights; squat, turn-of-the-century radiators warm the rooms while (sometimes smokey) log fires provide the atmosphere; white or pale shades of emulsion cover the walls apart from one surviving narrow strip showing the original painted decoration which would once have covered large areas; junk shop finds and family heirlooms furnish the rooms in a mixture of styles and periods. 'The only things we throw out,' says Limma, 'are modern.'

In 300 years a house has time to adapt to many styles. The decision facing conservationists is how much to strip back. The particularly Scottish austerity of bare stone walls was becoming outdated even in mid 17th century when interiors were acquiring a more classical look with plaster ceilings and wall linings. Some time in the 19th century Peffermill House was 'Victorianised' with raised doors and windows, smaller fireplaces, cornices and plaster ceilings. The cost of stripping it all back is prohibitive. 'We tried to concentrate on the Great Hall,' says Limma, 'to make it semi-authentic.'

When they took over, the Great Hall was lost in a succession of partitions which destroyed the original dimensions. Wooden beams were covered by plaster recently painted black and hidden by a suspended string ceiling, the walls were covered in lath and plaster and decorated with 'seedy' wallpaper.

*Opposite: a picturesque 17th-century Florentine inlaid cabinet, displays a vase of apple blossom from a tree in the garden; **Above left:** this painting in the Great Hall was copied from an Italian masterpiece in a Glasgow Gallery by Nick Groves-Raines' grandmother who studied painting with Whistler and Gauguin; **Above right:** the 19th century lingers on in the bathroom where a collection of coloured eye baths provides a splash of colour*

Main bedroom off the Great Hall where the bed and a small sofa are appropriately covered with needlework quilts; a 17th century wooden painted panel in the alcove shows Queen Elizabeth I with a group of Masked Players. On the chest is one of Limma Groves-Raines' collection of Doll's Houses, and standing out from the other interesting pieces in the room, a seascape after the Dutch School of Painting

Now the Great Hall stretches to something like its former length, stripped back to a bare simplicity. From behind the layers of paint, plaster and string, the original wooden ceiling has been exposed and repaired, missing beams replaced and the stone corbels destroyed by Victorian workmen copied by a local stone-mason and 'aged' with a needle gun. The walls have been taken back to rough plaster and behind the inappropriate Victorian fireplace the much larger fireplace with original stone lintel and right-hand jamb was discovered — a new left-hand jamb and hearth had to be made. Heavy pine doors at either end of the hall have been specially made — the irregularity of 17th century handmade nails has been achieved by Nick Groves-Raines with the help of horse-shoe nails and an anvil.

The 19th century lingers on in the bathroom partitioned off from the end of the hall near the main bedrooms, intimate in wood panelling and brass fittings and the one Victorian bath found intact after vandal attacks. The Victorian approach to light also remains. The 17th century window — unglazed, with shutters at the bottom and small leaded panes protected with iron bars in the top half — admits very little light. A good compromise is to use the heavier sections of early 18th century glazing bars — when money is available.

'One of the loveliest things about the house is the light,' says Limma. With windows facing different aspects in every room the quality of light changes through the day, sunlight floods the turnpike stair. The sense of light and space is enhanced by

The childrens' bedroom off the Great Hall is a delightful story-book room, with brass bed, patchwork, rocking horse and well loved books and toys. A Danish cupboard, made to look like a tallboy, is a useful receptacle in a house which is short of cupboards, as is the aumbry in the wall recess

bare painted floors with rugs, white or pale shades on the walls, white loose covers on the chairs and sofa in the Great Hall — 'easy to keep clean, you just throw them in the washing machine'.

Furnishing the fortified house turned out to be no problem. 'Over the years we have accumulated a lot of junk. The main difficulty is finding where to put family belongings in a house which was not built with cupboards — 'in those days obviously they just didn't have the clobber — so the attic is full of boxes of books, old prams and discarded toys !' But Edwardian and Georgian furniture fitted the rooms well. As the family spends a lot of time in the kitchen it was furnished with special care: open shelves rather than units — 'you just clean them twice a year' — and an enormous scrubbed pine table acquired after Holyrood Laundry burned down.

Heating, by gas, and cleaning present no difficulties either. But then the Groves-Raines/ Hannesdotir attitude does not consider the obstacles presented by the restoration of old houses: their spare time is spent working on a castle in the Highlands and an island bothy off the coast of Donegal.

'The driving force in all this is Nick,' says Limma, 'he has the energy and the vision. He just does not see problems in a project which someone else wouldn't dream of taking on. People ask how we can bear to sell a house we have worked on but I never feel anyone really owns a place. It's ours to live in for a short while and when we pass it on we hope it is better than when we found it.'

SAFE KEEP

When Schomberg Scott moved to Northfield House in Prestonpans he uncovered not only the history of the house but also its remarkable painted ceilings. *Nic Allen* visited him

'**A**place like this attracts its fair share of historical myths' observes Schomberg Scott wryly. 'Mary Queen of Scots slept in the house, but that was about twenty years before the place was built. And of course Bonnie Prince Charlie stayed here on the eve of the battle of Prestonpans — which would have entailed his obtaining a safe conduct from his opponent, Johnnie Cope, who was billeted literally across the road that night!'

Other equally charming stories about Northfield House have a truer ring to them. In the 1890s, for example, the owner decided to hang that most Victorian of furnishings, a large gas chandelier, from the ceiling of his dining room. His plumber cut a hole in the floor of the room above, and, when he looked at the underside of the piece of floorboard he had removed, found to his astonishment that it had a bunch of grapes painted on it. Half a century later Schomberg Scott, armed with a torch and mirror, probed further into that hole and what he saw provided him with the courage to pull down the demure Georgian plasterwork to reveal above it a series of ceilings ablaze with renaissance designs and colours.

Two hundred and fifty years of darkness have kept the ceilings away from the harmful effects of sunlight and the meddlesome attention of restorers. The bright patterns you see today at Northfield are little different from those commissioned by Joseph Marjoribanks at the beginning of the 17th century. And, says Schomberg Scott, while *he* owns the house no restorer is going to be allowed anywhere near them.

Northfield, he points out, has

always been in the hands of much the same sort of people — fairly well-to-do families who earned their living in Edinburgh but preferred life in the nearby countryside. Alterations and additions to the house over the centuries have been very much in line with the changing social needs and expectations of their class. What Marjoribanks bought in 1607 was a fairly straight-forward tower house with a Great Hall on the first floor reached by a narrow turnpike stair at its west end, which had been built by a local man, George Hamilton, a few years before. A mean winding stair may have been a suitable architectural expression for a society which still at the back of its mind saw buildings in terms of defence, but it was not the sort of approach likely to impress visitors to the home of a prosperous Edinburgh merchant. A grander, wider dog-leg stair was built at the other end of the hall leading down to the present front door which is still topped by the carved initials of Marjoribanks, his wife Marion Simpson, and the date 1611.

The extension which Marjoribanks built to the west of the house was equally typical of his day. The ground floor level contains a vaulted kitchen with, as Schomberg Scott points out with a grin, the painted arms of Marion Simpson (Marjoribanks clearly had a definite notion of where his wife belonged). On the first floor, adjoining the hall, the extension provided Marjoribanks' private quarters (a typical 17th century lay-out) with painted internal partitions as well as ceilings. Above this on the second floor sits the charming gallery, stretching narrowly across the width of the house.

As a status symbol for a renaissance merchant, the Great Hall with its brightly painted ceiling may have been quite the thing, but it was a bit too crude for genteel Georgian sensibilities. Soon after 1703, when the Marjoribanks sold Northfield to an Edinburgh legal family called Syme, the ceilings were plastered over and a cosier dining area partitioned off within the Great Hall. This 'cosification' was taken further a century later when the gallery ceiling which had probably been a painted cove was plastered over and the approach to these rooms upgraded once again by the transformation of the narrow turnpike into a wide, stylish Georgian curve. Northfield remained in the ownership of the Symes right up until 1896 when it passed to James McNeil, a mining engineer, from whose spinster daughter the Scotts purchased the house in 1953.

At the time Schomberg Scott was The National Trust for Scotland's architect and he naturally jumped at the opportunity of living in a house like Northfield. He made enquiries as soon as he heard rumours that it was coming on the market, rather to the surprise of Miss McNeil's lawyer — who had himself only just received instructions to sell. Miss McNeil had happy memories of growing up there, and this seems to have predisposed her to seeing the house pass to the Scotts with their young family.

It is easy to see that the great garden, the miniature turrets corbelled out from the corners of the gallery, the ever-present shapes and colours of the painted ceilings and walls would all be quite magical to a child. A Scott son still has one of the most exciting rooms (on the north side of Marjoribanks' private quarters) where 17th century beasts and motifs jostle in colourful anarchy with hi-tech equipment and rows of science fiction volumes.

Schomberg Scott's approach to Northfield has been an appropriately gentle one. There are a few reminders of his Trust connections — the Royal Arms on the hall wallpaper, for instance, were produced from a block which he had originally commissioned for papering at Falkland Palace. For the most part, however, homely family furnishings decorate the rooms, though a fair proportion of them — the oak furniture, the portrait engravings — are absolutely right for the house. He has no plans for future restoration, prefering to enjoy an existing interior which is forever casting up little examples of how it was used in the past. He points out the pattern of the flagstone floor in the old kitchen, or opens the door into one of the tiny turret rooms off the gallery to show that this is where he keeps his favourite books, just as the 17th century Scottish gentleman would have done.

'If you want to get hold of me, it's best to telephone in the evening,' he says — for the one place where improvement continues apace is in the magnificent garden and it is there, away from any inter-ruptions, that the Scotts tend to be found during the day. Thanks to the garden's development, the Marjoribanks' large, dark, vaulted

p.42: 'EXCEPT THE LORD BULD IN VANE BULDS MAN' reads the motto above the entrance to Northfield House which was added by Marjoribanks in 1611. Schomberg Scott's mind is on another aspect of the Creation as he prepares for a day tending Northfield's fine garden; p.43: Northfield unrestored. The naturalistic motifs are typical of Scottish beam-and-board ceiling painting; the colours, hidden from damaging light for over three centuries and untouched by restorers, retain much of their original vibrancy

Opposite, above left: *Marjoribanks' dog-legged stair;* ***Above right:*** *looking into the now partitioned Great Hall;* ***Below left and right:*** *when Schomberg Scott revealed the painted ceiling here, however, it was clear that it and the panelled dining room* ***(right)*** *were once part of the same room*

kitchen with its great fireplace and stone sink let into the wall, has taken on a new lease of life, overflowing with garden tools, bags of compost and orderly ranks of seed potatoes. The view of the tall, comfortable rear walls of Northfield with its steep pitched roof, tiny turrets and diminutive dovecote nestling high on the façade, has become as much a part of the Scotts' day-to-day existence as the remarkable rooms inside the house.

Above left: the well-lit gallery stretching the width of the original house, with its carved stone chimneypiece, retains a strong sense of what it was originally like, although it lost its original ceiling in the early 19th century; *Below left:* Internal wooden partitions at Northfield were originally painted in much the same way as the ceilings. A surviving example holds its own amid the colourful anarchy of a Scott son's room; *Opposite:* even the paraphernalia of the potting shed takes on a Vermeer-like aura in the light filtering into what was once Northfield's kitchen. Its grander days are still apparent in the large fireplace and the finely set flagstone floor

JXI 4972

GLASGOW'S SEAT

Kelburn Castle, the home of the Earl and Countess of Glasgow, is enjoying a second renaissance at the centre of a thriving country park. *Ian Gow* discovered that the original renaissance wing of the house has a split personality. Behind the austere exterior lies an early flowering of Scottish classical style

The Boyles of Kelburn have displayed an unusual but consistent approach to their home. Instead of adapting it to accommodate the latest ideas of comfort, they have preferred to add afresh, leaving the old intact. The result is a Y-shaped block, comprising three separate 'houses': a James VI tower house, a William and Mary country house and a Victorian wing. The three meet in a 'Clapham Junction' outside the kitchen door, where an already contorted passage has to dodge around a circular tower. Here amid the entrails of his house, Patrick Boyle, tenth Earl of Glasgow, demonstrates a further layer to visitors, since his practised eye can detect that the rectangular tower is an extension of a much earlier square keep.

The first-time visitor to Kelburn must tear himself away from such antiquarian speculation and even from the Victorian wing, with its skied billiard room, for the real glory of the castle is the William and Mary addition. It is a striking mixture of the atavistic with the progressively modern. A line of 'anglophile baroque' staterooms lie concealed behind a façade designed in the last vestiges of the Scottish tower house vernacular. This marriage of architectural styles is a fitting reflection of its builder, for the central event in the life of David Boyle was his successful conclusion of the Treaty of Union in 1707.

An astute politician, an ardent supporter of the Protestant succession and a protégé of the powerful Duke of Queensberry, his career was loaded with honours and in 1703 he was raised to the peerage as the first Earl of Glasgow. He seems to have held equally decided views on architecture, but, sadly, his building activities are inadequately documented except for a confusing building contract of 1692 with the mason, Thomas Caldwell, which is still in the house.

To express his prestige and house his grand friends, the new work had to reflect current thinking through symmetry of composition and contain an axially aligned suite of rooms equipped with such up-to-date technology as the sash window. His decision to follow the style of the old tower and copy earlier features may have been dictated by a desire to stress his family's antiquity. His titles might be new, but there had been Boyles at Kelburn since the 12th century.

Thus for his frontispiece, where a classical architect like Sir William Bruce or James Smith would have designed a temple front with orders, Lord Glasgow cobbled together and drilled into symmetry a reworking of such traditional elements as crow-stepped gables, chimneys and an heraldic panel over the principal door. To give an ornamental flourish, the prosaic rain-water pipe became an extravaganza in leadwork. Although it divides, in order to observe the necessary symmetry, it seems to owe more to heraldry than architecture and culminates in a three-dimensional, and rather dotty, double-headed eagle over the entrance — a spirited rendering of the family crest. These marked architectural failings, however, are the source of its very considerable charm. MacGibbon and Ross, connoisseurs of the castellated, who visited in July 1886, pronounced it 'homely and quaint'.

There is nothing uncouth about the plan — that of a miniature palace which was right up to date. In combination, the contrast of exterior and interior is curiously schizophrenic. In such uncertainty, if we may read the man in his architecture, it comes as no surprise that this apparent pillar of the Protestant succession toppled in 1714, when despite vigorous protestations to the contrary he came under suspicion of being a Jacobite. His political career came to an end and remaining energies were devoted to his estates at Kelburn, where he died in 1733.

What makes the William and Mary work remarkable today is that through the chances of inheritance it remained unaltered. In the course of a series of marriages, subsequent Earls of Glasgow built up an impressive collection of estates and from the late 18th century Kelburn lost its primacy as their seat, first to Hawkhead at Paisley, and then to Crawford Priory in Fife. Until its renaissance in 1886 the only evidence of the passing of one and a half centuries seems to have been a set of Georgian Chippendale bookcases and the early Victorian paintwork in the drawing room. Kelburn's revival was a direct consequence of the sixth Earl's misfortunes.

Though revered as a pious benefactor of the Scottish Episcopalian church, whose buildings include the Cathedral at Perth, a private chapel at Crawford Priory and the college and Cathedral of the Isles at Millport on Cumbrae, where he had his summer residence, he is less charitably remembered within the family circle as the Earl who brought the family to the brink of bankruptcy. To ease his difficulties he broke the entail on his estates and Kelburn was auctioned. Happily it was saved by his kinsman, David Boyle of Shewalton, who was also his heir. Lord Glasgow had no sons.

When the future seventh Earl brought life back to Kelburn, its architecture was already beginning to be appreciated. It was, however, too early for an authentic archaeological approach such as Sir Robert Lorimer pioneered, and David Boyle's renovations possess an 'artistic' strain noticeable in the wrought-iron hinges to his new front door, the choice of grates fitted to old chimneypieces, the light fittings and perhaps — most ostentatiously — by the Morris textiles and paper in the new dining room wing, sited to take full advantage of the view. The architect for the

Above: the Great Staircase is
dignified by panelling and its
heavy wooden balusters imitate
the stone baluster at Holyrood,
but the formality is softened by
19th century oriental rugs sewn
together to form a continuous
patchwork stair-carpet; **Below:**
a lobby on the first floor of the
tower leads from the circular
stair. Originally this may have
formed part of the first Earl's
private suite

Above: the first Earl's Great Dining Room, now the drawing room, incorporates architectural panelling with Corinthian pilasters but the naivety of its execution saves it from over-formality. The frieze is in carved wood and it bristles with thistles over the doors. The drawing room is the only room at Kelburn with a mid-Victorian flavour, since it was re-decorated around 1850 with gold stencilling to a formula devised by David Ramsay Hay, a protégé of Sir Walter Scott. This decoration which quotes from the family heraldry may be by Hay's pupil, Thomas Bonnar, who worked extensively for the sixth Earl at Crawford Priory. The principal door is now concealed by a superb baroque glass with bevelled plates

Opposite: a detail of the very large sash windows of the original Great Dining Room; *Next page:* the drawing room chimneypiece with its Corinthian pilasters frames an early topographical view of Kelburn Castle and estate. The lobby on the left leads through into the State Bedroom

restoration is not known but the Australian historian Donald Ellsmore has found a reference to the Glasgow firm of Guthrie & Wells acting as decorators.

By 1886 the more important historic possessions at Kelburn had been auctioned or scattered to the Glasgows' seats and the house seems to be furnished largely with the pictures and comfortable furniture from Shewalton, which was sold. The interiors are therefore informal.

Kelburn's old-fashioned air begins with the survival of the first Earl's forecourt and gate piers which once enclosed his parterres. An early photograph shows rampant and unkempt box hedges, which proves how fully Kelburn escaped late Georgian notions of landscaping. The Earl's interior architectural effects were reserved for his *piano nobile*, and oddly the front door merely opened into a narrow lobby leading to the stair.

This has now been enlarged into a hall where a gilded Whytock & Reid mirror reflects the gravel path and gate piers when the door is opened, and two insignificant corner chimney-pieces bear witness to the former partition. The great staircase has heavy balusters and is dignified by panelling.

The landing at the stair head was meant to open on a process-ional axis into the Great Dining Room in the centre of the house, whose grand dimensions would provide a contrast. In the Victorian period however, it became the principal drawing room and perhaps in an attempt to defeat draughts, the main door was closed. It is typical of Kelburn that this was effected by the simple means of locking the door without any structural alteration.

We must now enter through the smaller secondary door from an adjoining passage. Approach-ing from the corner however, one is even more aware of the impressive scale of the room which is flooded with light by the sashes in three of its sides. Perhaps because these are so ambitiously large, only the lower section of each window-frame is counter-weighted to slide, the upper lights apparently having been never meant to open.

The effect of the panelling here, with its applied Corinthian order is very architectural, but its naivety saves it from pomposity. The frieze is of carved wood rather than plaster, which gives a soapy, rather than a crisp, effect and it bristles into thistles over the principal doors. Alone of the rooms at Kelburn, the drawing room is stamped with a layer of distinctively Scottish Victorian taste since the panelling has been stencilled and the room is finished in the 'Louis' style of the 1840s.

The first Earl's stress on symmetry demanded two equal chimneypieces in the end walls but Victorian comfort demanded the supremacy of the innermost, which was promoted into a double decker mantelpiece with the addition of antique carvings.

We now resume the process-ional axis which leads on into the original drawing room, whose handsome bolection moulded chimneypiece is importantly flanked by Corinthian pilasters so that it closes the vista through the Great Dining Room. The over-mantel contains a remarkable early 'bird's eye view' showing Kelburn and its inhabitants, both human and animal in the first Earl's day. It is a fascinating record, with many unexpected details such as the correct heraldic tincture painted on the lead eagle above the door. Facing this are two of the set of handsome mid-Georgian book-cases whose quality is reflected in the confident profiles of their upswept cornices and swelling bracket-feet.

Beyond the drawing room there is a temporary pause in a lobby to gain space for the back stairs before we enter the state bedchamber. Pilasters flanking

the chimneypiece once again produce an architectural effect but this stab at grandeur is diminished by the plaster rosettes in the cornice which would be happier on an iced wedding cake than in their intended role as components of an architectural order. Because this room enjoys a spectacular view across the Firth of Clyde and Cumbrae to the mountains of Argyll, it became a sitting room in the seventh Earl's renovation and the fireplace was altered. The position of the state bed is revealed by the blocking of the windows to the court with a run of panelling. The crewel work introduced by Dorothea, wife of the seventh Earl, is perfectly in tune with a William and Mary ambience. The closet lies behind the service stair which also gave access to a servant's room.

The splendours of this state apartment would be sufficient for any house, but at Kelburn we still have two other 'houses' to explore. Today country house buffs are as likely to be more excited by the painted oilcloth — an early form of linoleum which lines a cupboard in imitation Roman mosaic — than by the William Morris curtains and wallpaper in the Victorian dining room.

Doubtless many other exciting discoveries remain to be made.

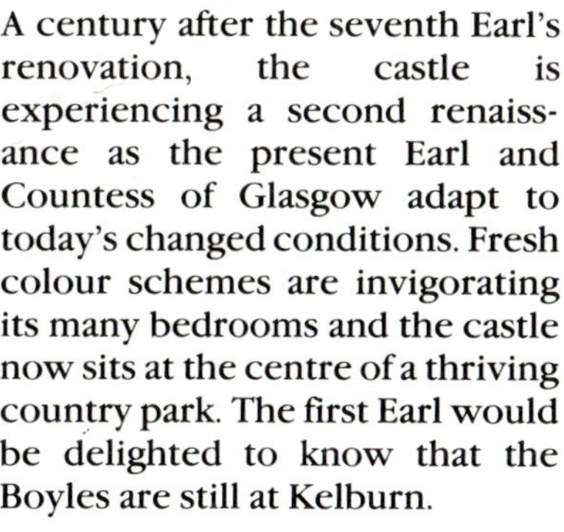

Opposite: the State Bedroom is now an informal sitting room which commands spectacular views across the Firth of Clyde. The fireplace is late-Victorian. However, its neo-baroque style harmonises well with the first Earl's panelling with its handsome Corinthian pilasters, as do the crewel-work hangings — all preserve an old-fashioned air in the principal rooms; Above: at first glance, the detailing of the State Bedroom cornice seems architecturally correct. On closer inspection, it appears engagingly naive, as though the plasterer was over-reaching himself and found it hard to contain the unruly rosettes within the architectural framework

A century after the seventh Earl's renovation, the castle is experiencing a second renaissance as the present Earl and Countess of Glasgow adapt to today's changed conditions. Fresh colour schemes are invigorating its many bedrooms and the castle now sits at the centre of a thriving country park. The first Earl would be delighted to know that the Boyles are still at Kelburn.

NORTHERN STARS

The tower houses of North-east Scotland —
'The Castle Country' — have a timeless and
poetic beauty. Some of the best examples,
including Craigievar and Crathes, are in the
care of The National Trust for Scotland. But
the Trust cares for gardens too, and the Great
Garden of Pitmedden is a fascinating example
of the formal gardens designed for
renaissance castles

*Above: Crathes contains splendid painted ceilings
and treasure gifted by Robert the Bruce; **Opposite:**
the Long Gallery at Crathes has a rare oak-panelled
ceiling. The laird's court sometimes met in this
splendid room*

Crathes was largely the work of a remarkable family of master masons called Bell, who worked in the Aberdeen area and probably also built Midmar, Castle Fraser and Craigievar. Three coats-of-arms on the south wall include that of the Bells' clients, Alexander Burnett and Janet Hamilton, the founders of Crathes who married in 1543; their great-grandson Alexander and his wife Katherine Gordon, the first inhabitants of Crathes; and the Royal Arms of Scotland which proclaim Crathes as a royal barony.

It was the young Alexander who supervised the finishing of the magnificent turreted top storey of Crathes and ordered the painting of the ceilings which reveal the breadth of his moral and artistic interest. The painted ceilings, restored in the 19th century, are one of the delights of Crathes. Its greatest treasure is the Horn of Leys which hangs over the Hall fireplace. It is said to have been given to the first Burnett of Leys (an Anglo-Saxon who moved to the Border country with Norman English families, and later settled in the North-east) by Robert the Bruce in 1323 as a symbol of his authority as a Royal Forester.

The Long Gallery, stretching the full width of the top floors of the castle, is unique. Its rare, oak-panelled ceiling is one of very few of its kind to survive. The finely cut ceiling panels are over-laid with a pattern of moulded ribs in diamond and oblong formations, punctuated by coats-of-arms and recurrent motifs of Burnett holly leaves and the Horn of Leys. The centre rib displays six shields belonging to the first baronet; the King of Scotland, his overlord; the Marquis of Hamilton, his cousin; Lord Dunfermline, the Chancellor of Scotland, his close friend; Alexander Burnett, his

Above: the laird's bedroom at Crathes has lost its painted ceiling but it boasts a magnificent carved oak bed which is associated with the Aberdeen school of woodcarving;
Opposite: The Great Hall of Craigievar is one of the most remarkable rooms in Scotland

great-grandfather; and Gilbert Burnett, Bishop of Salisbury.

Meetings of the laird's court were sometimes held in this room instead of the Hall, and the 17th century chairs and oak tables have been set out as if for this event. The floral marquetry cabinet is English and dates from about 1685. The remaining woodwork in the Long Gallery is 19th century.

The laird's bedroom has lost its painted wooden ceiling but boasts a splendid carved oak bed made for Alexander and Katherine Burnett. It is dated 1594 and decorated with carved holly leaves, the Horn of Leys and boars' heads. Carving of such quality in this part of Scotland is associated with the Aberdeen school of woodcarving.

CRAIGIEVAR

Even in a country and a county famed for its tower houses, Craigievar stands out as the foremost example of the baronial style which was Scotland's finest contribution to European domestic architecture. Although its profusion of gables and turrets inspired many 19th century architects, fortunately Craigievar escaped 'Victorianisation' and remains very much as it was in 1626, the year of its completion.

The National Trust for Scotland re-harled the castle and repaired the roof in 1973, ten years after it was acquired from Lord Sempill. Evidence uncovered during the re-harling suggests that the Great Hall assumed its present form between 1610 and 1626 when it was owned by William Forbes of Menie (nicknamed 'Danzig Willie' from the fortune he made from trading with the Baltic countries).

The medieval Hall is one of the finest and most remarkable rooms in Scotland. Its soaring vaulted ceiling, massive fireplace with elaborate overmantel plasterwork, screens and musicians' gallery capture the spirit of Craigievar, which marries ancient and traditional forms with renaissance expression.

The splendid decoration was the work of journeyman plasterers who travelled widely and worked in Scotland and England in the early 17th century. The moulds used at Craigievar were also used at Bromley-by-Bow in 1606, Glamis in 1620 and Muchalls in 1624.

On either side of the central pendant are the arms of William Forbes and his wife Margaret Woodward. Above the fireplace, with its massive granite lintel, is one of the most magnificent examples of British heraldry. The laird of Craigievar, as a tenant-in-chief of the Crown was entitled to display his achievement and his authority to administer justice over his lands in the King's name at barony courts.

Contemporary with the plaster ceiling is the oak panelling, probably the work of local craftsmen.

Behind the screens meals would be made ready for serving on the 17th century oak dining table which, like much of the furniture in the castles and country houses of the North-east, originated in the Low Countries. The large armchairs, now covered in Forbes tartan, were made in the 19th century and the carpet was woven to match in 1970. A collection of studio pottery displayed in the room was purchased for Craigievar by Cecilia, Lady Sempill, and includes work by Bernard Leach and Michael Cardew. These contemporary pieces accord perfectly with the strong forms and plasterwork decoration of the Great Hall.

PITMEDDEN

The Great Garden of Pitmedden was founded by Sir Alexander Seton, second son of John Seton of Pitmedden. The lintel above the garden door bears the carved inscription *Fundat 2 May 1675* with the initials of Alexander and his wife, Dame Margaret Lauder. He was knighted by Charles II in 1664, and when he inherited Pitmedden divided his time between the estate, his new garden and the Law. In 1677 he took his seat as Lord Pitmedden, a Senator of the College of Justice and became a Baronet of Nova Scotia in 1683. He represented Aberdeenshire in the Scottish Parliament, but his opposition to the re-establishment of Roman Catholicism offended James VII and II who had him removed from the bench.

Sir William Bruce of Balcaskie, the great Scottish architect, was an acquaintance of Sir Alexander Seton. His house and garden at Kinross, completed in 1690, were influenced by Bruce's admiration for the work of the French architect Le Vau and the designer Le Notre, whose work came together in the chateau of Vaux-le-Vicomte near Paris, which Bruce visited.

It is reasonable to suppose that Bruce's enthusiasm influenced the design of Pitmedden. But there were other patterns more closely at hand to offer inspiration to the Scottish laird. According to Elizabeth Haldane in her book *Scots Gardens in Old Times,* over a hundred great houses with formal gardens existed in the area around Edinburgh alone. The Palace of Holyroodhouse, rebuilt by Sir William Bruce for Charles II in 1671, had an elaborate garden laid out in geometrical patterns.

When it accepted Pitmedden in 1951, The National Trust for Scotland intended to re-create the Great Garden in its

Opposite: the exterior of Craigievar, the foremost example of Scottish baronial style, remains very much as it was in 1626 when it was completed

entirety. This was a daunting task, since Sir Alexander's original three acres had become a kitchen garden. But the architectural skeleton remained: the pavilions, walls and stairs provided a stone framework for the vision of a team of experts which went to work under the guidance of Dr James S. Richardson.

The garden was marked out in four great rectangles, or parterres, outlined by three miles of boxwood hedges and divided by turf paths. Three of the designs come from Gordon of Rothiemay's drawings of the garden of Holyroodhouse and the fourth depicts Sir Alexander's coat-of-arms, flanked by a saltire and thistle.

Forty thousand annual plants, raised in glasshouses and frames are planted out in May to colour the designs of the four parterres. Some of the annuals are gradually being replaced by perennials while restoration work never ceases on the marvellous amalgam of parterres, buttresses, herbaceous borders, grass and fruit trees which make the Great Garden, contained by its staunch granite walls, a place of timeless beauty and historical importance.

Aerial view of the Great Garden of Pitmedden, founded in 1675, which contains forty thousand plants and three miles of box hedging

The articles above were edited from The National Trust for Scotland's publications, Crathes, Craigievar and Pitmedden. All three booklets are available at Trust shops. Information about the Trust can be obtained at Trust properties or from The National Trust for Scotland, 5 Charlotte Square, Edinburgh, EH2 4DU.

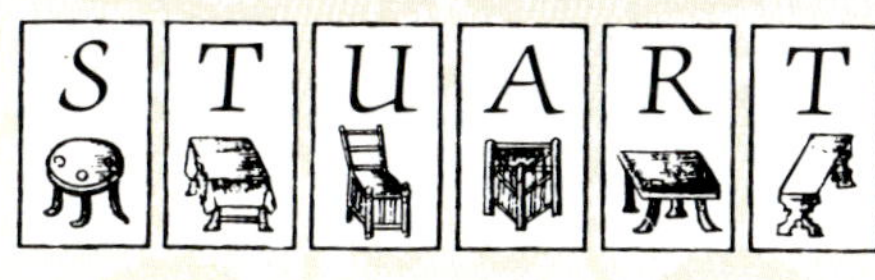

Above:

An oak carved and painted Chest, made in Dorset, circa 1650. (Reference: Oak Furniture-The British Tradition by Victor Chinnery, page 136.)

A very fine Yorkshire Armchair, carved and inlaid, of exceptional colour and patina.

Always a large selection of early oak furniture in stock.

Left:

A handmade copy of the 'Corbet' bed now on display in the Victoria and Albert Museum.

Specialist designers and manufacturers, covering all aspects of early English furniture, interior design and decoration.

Send £3 for a colour brochure

STUART INTERIORS, Barrington Court, Barrington, Ilminster, Somerset. TA19 0NQ Tel. (0460) 40349 *Open: Mon-Sat 9.30am-5pm*

Soft Furnishings by Design Studio

We can offer a full upholstery service from supply of new furniture to recovering your old suite to give it a new lease of life. We are also able to offer an antique restoration service and with clever use of modern and traditional fabrics can provide a distinctively superior result with superb craftmanship and beautiful finish.

Our furnishing fabrics can be used in most interiors and we have available an extensive range including flameproofed fabrics for contract applications.

Few things affect a rooms appearance more than the curtains, and their style and colour are of utmost importance. We offer an extensive range of curtain fabrics in the best of European designs from simple to sumptuous. A visit to our showroom where we have thousands of samples is an enlightening experience.

When the talk is about the best in interior design, Design Studio is the first to be mentioned. With our imaginative use of furnishing fabrics, our distinctive style could also be yours.

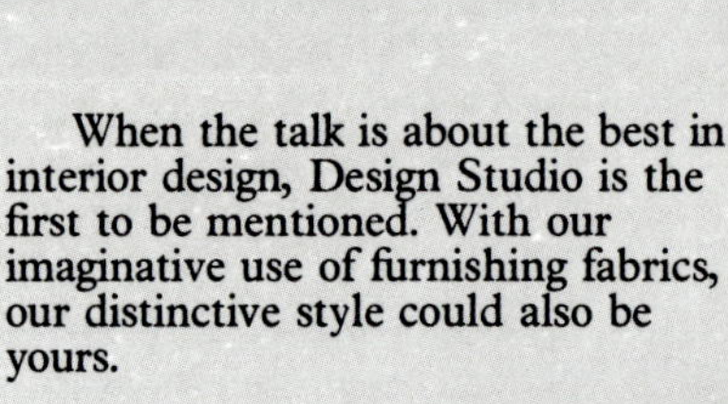

Hand finished curtains, flamboyant festoon blinds, traditional roman blinds, pelmets, sofas, armchairs and footstools can all be created by our experienced staff. Our comprehensive made-to-measure service offers a variety of soft furnishings.

Bath Street and Bridge Street · Aberdeen · Telephone 0224 594684

CHAIRS OF THE TRADES

The collection of French-inspired *cacqueteuse* chairs at Trinity Hall in Aberdeen, and other examples of these extraordinary oak armchairs at Provand's Lordship and the Burrell Collection in Glasgow, demonstrate that renaissance lairds and merchants appreciated high standards of craftsmanship in the decoration of their interiors
Text: *Victor Chinnery*

This early 17th century Scottish oak cacqueteuse, inlaid with fruitwood arabesques and the initials IG was sold by Christies in May 1987

Aberdeen was a major centre of furniture-making in renaissance Scotland, and today the city houses an important collection of armchairs, known as *cacqueteuse* chairs. A small collection of furniture of this type can also be seen at Provand's Lordship in Glasgow which was put together earlier this century, and the Burrell Collection contains three fine examples of *cacqueteuse* chairs.

The seaports of eastern Scotland — Leith, Dundee, Montrose, Abderdeen — supported thriving mercantile communities in the 16th and 17th centuries, and the furniture produced in these centres is still to be found scattered in great country houses and castles throughout the region.

Unfortunately it has not yet been possible to analyse the nuances of individual local styles in the simple jointed armchairs in oak and pine which are known and include several pine examples from Stonehaven and one from Lumphanan, dated 1688. These chairs suggest a vivid but crude tradition of furniture-making in the countryside and the fishing ports, which utilised local woods.

It was as a direct result of cultural contacts made with France in the reign of Mary, Queen of Scots, that a preference for *cacqueteuse* armchairs became firmly established in Scotland. These finer examples of the Franco-Scottish type are, however, associated with the

DECORATORS & FURNISHERS
ARCHITECTURAL SERVICES
COMPLETE SCHEMES
BANKS
BOARDROOMS
TOWN & COUNTRY HOUSES
CABINETMAKERS
POLISHERS
RESTORATIONS
CUSTOM-MADE FURNITURE
ANTIQUES
REPRODUCTIONS
LIGHT FITTINGS
UPHOLSTERY FABRICS
CURTAINS
CARPETS
ORIENTAL CARPETS
CHURCH FURNISHINGS
SPECIALIST PAINTERS
MARBLING
GILDING
WALLPAPERS

BY APPOINTMENT
TO HER MAJESTY THE QUEEN
DECORATORS & FURNISHERS

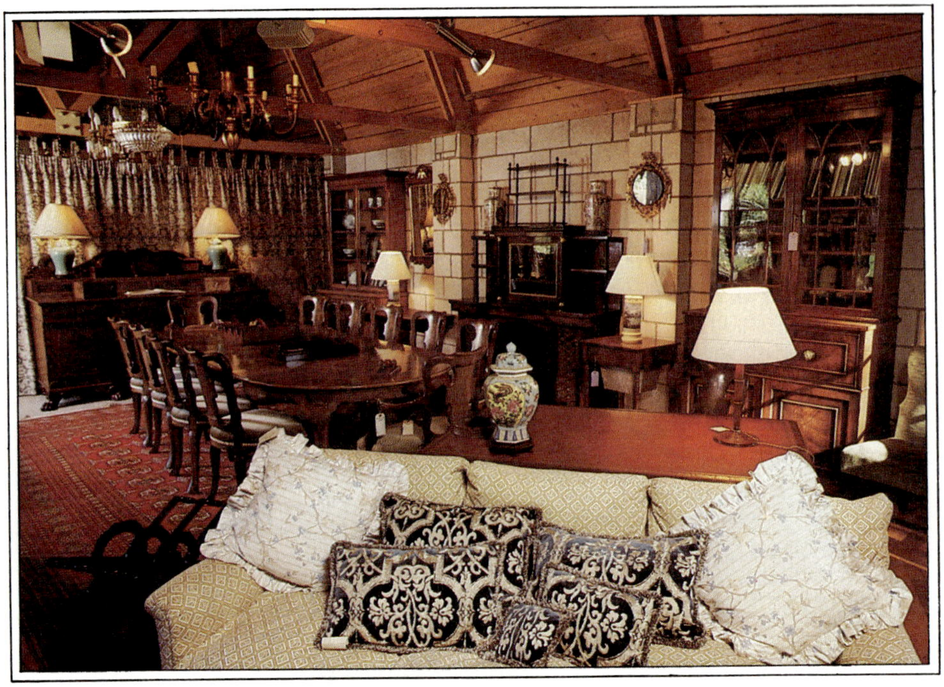

WHYTOCK & REID
SUNBURY HOUSE · BELFORD MEWS
EDINBURGH
Telephone 031-226 4911 EH4 3DN

Complete Design & Installation Service of Kitchens and Bathrooms

Compehensive Range of Ceramic wall and floor tiles to complement your interior

KITCHEN SPECIALISTS ASSOCIATION MEMBERS

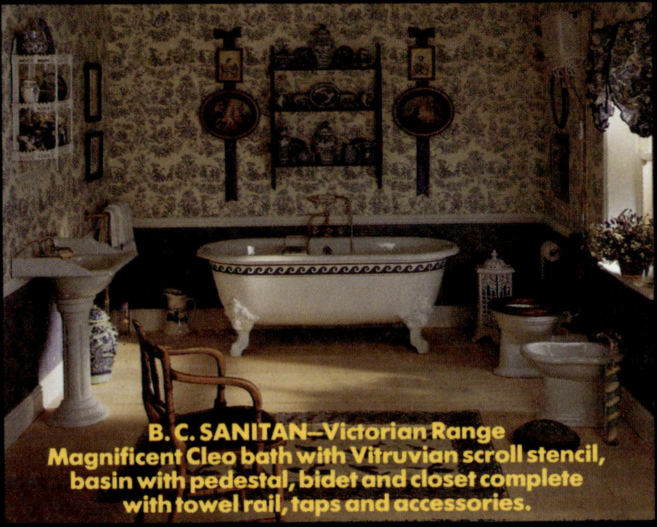

B. C. SANITAN—Victorian Range
Magnificent Cleo bath with Vitruvian scroll stencil, basin with pedestal, bidet and closet complete with towel rail, taps and accessories.

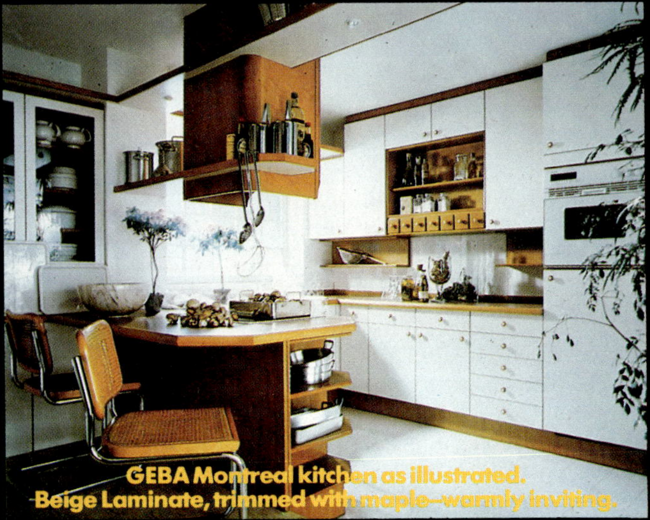

GEBA Montreal kitchen as illustrated.
Beige Laminate, trimmed with maple—warmly inviting.

CONTINENTAL CERAMICS
(KITCHEN & BATHROOM CENTRE)
LTD.

31/35 MARSHALL STREET
EDINBURGH EH8 9BJ
Tel 031-667 6725

Opening hours: MON, TUES, WED, FRID & SAT
9am-5.30pm, THURS 9am-7.30pm

urban workshops, and notably those of Aberdeen and Edinburgh.

The ancient city of Aberdeen, rich and influential at the beginning of the 17th century, housed one of the four Scottish universities, and served a large hinterland in the North-east. At Trinity Hall, headquarters of the Incorporated Trades of Aberdeen, a group of *cacqueteuse* chairs was assembled in the 17th century. As might be expected, the chairs used there represented the finest products then available in the city.

The guild organisation comprised the following trades: hammermen, bakers, wrights and coopers, barber-surgeons, tailors, shoe-makers, weavers and fleshers. No doubt, if it becomes possible to identify the makers of any of these chairs, they will be numbered among the members of the Wrights and Coopers Incorporation. The chairs were donated to mark their terms of office by Deacons of each trade, or by the Master of the Company. An inventory of 1696 lists a total of twenty-three chairs, of which fifteen can still be identified. Some examples are as follows:

Hammermen.
ane cheer gifted by Matthew Guild, armourer.
ane cheer gifted by Patrick Whyt, hookmaker, Deacon Conveener, 1690.
Wrights and Coopers.
ane cheer gifted by Jerome Blak, couper, 1574. (A box base armchair, not a cacqueteuse).
ane cheer gifted by William Ord, wright, Deacon Conveener, 1635.
Taylziours.
ane cheer gifted by Thomas Cordyn, tayler, Deacon Conveener, 1627.
Fleshers.
ane cheer gifted by Andrew Watson, Deacon.

ane cheer marked WP coft to the Hospital.

Andrew Watson's chair, noted above, has a claim to distinction in the very material from which it is made. This is probably the earliest dated piece of mahogany furniture of British make (1661), though I recently discovered an undated chair in Brazilian mahogany (bulletwood) which appears to have been made for the Roope family of Dartmouth, circa 1617.

The timber of Andrew Watson's chair is extremely close-grained and hard, of a slight reddish hue, with a bright patination. Over the years it has taken a good polish, and the wear has been slight but even. Oak and pine are the usual timbers in Scottish furniture (whether native or imported from Scandinavia), but the presence of mahogany in Aberdeen at this date should not be a surprise. 'Spanish' or 'Jamaica' wood was well known by the middle of the 17th century, and a few planks might easily have found their way into the busy port of Aberdeen from Spain or France.

Through most of the 17th century, chairs still exhibited the same spirited refinement of carving that is seen on the earlier work; but there is little evidence that this excellence was carried on into the 18th century. Chairs dated later in the 17th century show a decline in the former high traditions of carving in urban Aberdeen, though the joinery is still solid and well formed.

The furniture at Trinity Hall, Provand's Lordship and the Burrell Collection provides us with a sturdy reminder that the renaissance landowners and burghers of east and north-east Scotland appreciated the highest standards of craftsmanship in interior decoration.

TURKISH TROVE

Rug-restorer, *John Maclean*, finds evidence of carpets in 16th and 17th century paintings, wills and inventories, including 'sevin greit and nine small' which belonged to Mary, Queen of Scots, and 'twa auld and worn away' to her mother, Mary of Guise

The Sheffield Portrait of Mary, Queen of Scots, 1578. She is shown standing on a 'small pattern Holbein' carpet;
Opposite: *Early 17th century portrait of the 3rd Earl of Lothian standing on what appears to be a copy of a Turkish carpet.*

Carpets were treasured in the renaissance period. They were walked on as little as possible and inventories describe them as : *cubborde carpettes, wyndowe carpettes, table carpettes, hanging carpettes, foot carpettes and tapies.* These valuable and colourful rugs provided artists of the day with rich backgrounds for portraits of Royal and titled patrons.

The 1578 Sheffield portrait which hangs in the Scottish National Portrait Gallery depicts Mary, Queen of Scots standing on a 'small pattern Holbein' carpet. Ottoman

WILLIAM EARLE OF
LOTHIAN

*The Strathmore carpet, dated 1620, is one of the earliest
carpets known to have come from a Scottish house*

carpets like this were popular in Europe from the 15th to
the 17th centuries, and were produced around Ushak in
Turkey.

Formal portraiture offers a rich source for research
into Oriental carpets. In fact certain carpet types are named
after the artist who favoured, or had access to, a particular
design; thus, 'small pattern Holbein', 'large pattern Holbein'
and 'Lotto'. This system of identification solves certain
problems, but can mislead the unaware. Large pattern

Holbein carpets, for example, appear in paintings long after the artist's death.

In the interpretation of the Sheffield portrait, too, care is needed. Since Mary Stuart was held captive in England in 1578, the carpet in the painting cannot be identified as belonging to the Royal Wardrobe of Scotland. Mary left Scotland with no possessions, and it is possible that the carpet belonged to her custodian for fifteen years, the Earl of Shrewsbury. Other evidence suggests that the portrait, and several other versions of it, were not painted until the early 17th century (perhaps as keepsakes commissioned for loyal supporters after Mary's death).

A second painting, in the Palace of Holyroodhouse, shows the Countess of Lennox (Lord Darnley's mother) standing on what is thought to be the first representation of a Lotto rug in British portraiture. Lotto rugs like this, also produced in the Ushak region, are found in paintings from the early 16th to late 17th centuries. At the time of the painting (around 1560) the Countess of Lennox was living on her English estate of Temple Newsam, a fact which raises questions about whether the carpet belonged there or travelled from Scotland with her as part of her 'removing garderobe'.

The earliest direct linking of carpets with Scottish houses is possible through two owned by the Duke of Buccleuch, dated 1584 and 1585, and the Strathmore carpet of 1620, which was a table carpet. They were, however, produced around Norwich. Hand-knotted and piled English reproduction Turkey-work carpets like these, their jute warps and wefts distinguishing them from Oriental carpets, grew in popularity throughout the 17th century.

The largest source of untapped information concerning the history of the Oriental carpet in Scotland is contained in documents like wills and inventories. Donald King, the former keeper of textiles and costume in the Victoria and Albert Museum, has opened up the field through his work on the Royal Inventories, compiled on the death of Henry VIII in 1547. This provides us with the largest documented collection of Oriental carpets in the 16th century. While 437 of the 801 carpets described are classed as 'Turkish', it has to be remembered that the term referred to the Ottoman Empire which embraced the main trade links with Venice and the West.

Scotland cannot boast inventories on anything like this scale, yet there is mention of carpets in a number of listings. One of the most interesting inventories relates to Mary of Guise and notes: *'Twa auld Tapies of Turquie worn away'*. The inventory of the Royal Wardrobe and Jewelhouse of Mary, Queen of Scots, lists: *'Saxtene turkie tapies contening sevin greit and nine small'*. And an inventory taken of the furnishings destroyed at Kirk o' Field (in the explosion after which Lord Darnley was found dead) presented to Mary for her counter-signature notes *'a little Turkie carpet and a chamber-pot'*.

Edward Atkinson Hornel 1864-1933

Sir William MacTaggart P.P.R.S.A. 1903-1981

George Turner 1843-1910

William Marshall Brown R.S.A. 1863-1936

Robert Gemmel Hutchison R.S.A. 1855-1936   John McGhie G.I. 1867-1949   Alexander Ignatius Roche R.S.A. 1861-1921

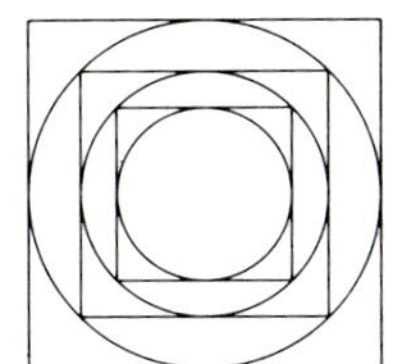

Crichton Lang, Willis + Galloway
Architects

3 Walker Street
Edinburgh EH3 7JY
Scotland UK

Telephone 031-226 7031

Experts in conservation, restoration
and interior design.
Some of our recently completed works include:
Newton Don House, Kelso
(illustrated above)
Thirlestane Castle, Lauder.
Lochnell Castle, Argyll.
New Lanark.

FESTIVAL EXHIBITION

ALBERTO MORROCCO, RSA, RSW

THE SCOTTISH GALLERY
7 August-2 September

FINE ART DEALERS   ESTABLISHED 1842

94 GEORGE STREET · EDINBURGH · Tel: 031-225 5955

Weddell & Thomson
Architects Interior Designers

OFFICES OF THE PRACTICE AT HUGHENDEN HOUSE

GENERAL SERVICE

Established in 1932, the practice offers a comprehensive Architectural and Interior Design service in both commercial and residential sectors.

Budget management, strict cost control and site supervision are part of the standard service.

SPECIALIST SERVICES

The Partnership offers a specialist service of Interior Design to the hotel and leisure industry, an experienced knowledge of Licencing Court procedure and liaison with Local Authority departments such as Planning, Environmental Health, Police, Fire and Building Control.

PARAPHERNALIA INCORPORATED

The Practice can add the finishing touches to an interior by accessorising with antiques and bric-a-brac through its subsidiary company, Paraphernalia Incorporated.

Weddell & Thomson
Architects Interior Designers

Hughenden House Hughenden Road Glasgow
G12 9XP Telephone: 041-334 1171/2/3

- *Have a top quality Continental kitchen and save money.*
- *Don't miss this opportunity to acquire a top quality hand-finished kitchen from France's No. 1 manufacturer -ARTHUR BONNET.*
- *The very special style and charm that is unique to French kitchens can be yours at a price you can afford.*
- *AND we will design your kitchen FREE.*
- *For a FREE fixed price quotation, phone:- (0592) 715244 or (after hours) 0592 712343*

SEND FOR A FREE BROCHURE
Forster's Design Studio
Sea Road, Methilhill, Leven
(Opp. Old Toll Hotel)

SYLVIA LAWSON JOHNSTON–INTERIOR DESIGN
35 ALBERT STREET
ABERDEEN
Tel. 0224 640690

You are invited to view our exclusive showroom displaying our latest selection of quality Reproduction and Traditional Furniture and Furnishings.

59/73 JAMES STREET, BRIDGETON, GLASGOW G40 1BZ
Tel: 041-554 7281

Business Hours:
Monday – Saturday
9am till 5pm
Sundays
12 noon till 5pm

Woolfsons of James Street Ltd.

SCOTS RENAISSANCE STYLE

Scottish renaissance interiors were brightly coloured and decorated. Thanks to the work of experts like *Victor Chinnery* it is possible to piece together the evidence for how this effect was achieved

The restored barrel vaulted ceiling of Moubray House is dated 1600 and shows traces of original painting. The distinctive window design was modelled on a similar one at Jerviswood House, Lanarkshire

It is remarkable that most of us so readily accept what we are shown as representing how things looked, however many centuries ago, when visiting an historic interior. But the reality is that it takes a lively imagination to conjure up the rich and colourful character of the interior decoration of renaissance rooms. The twin qualities of colour and freshness are invariably missing from modern reconstructions of 16th or 17th century interiors. In fact, to create a truly historical reconstruction would require taking radical steps to make new furniture in the correct style and put it together with fresh paint, new metalwork, pottery and freshly woven fabrics.

Newly finished oak furniture and woodwork is, after all, a pale biscuit colour and not the dark, richly patinated colour we see today. So we who admire the softening and darkening effect of age should try to imagine the appearance of fabrics, paints and polished wood when they were new and formed the all-important physical background to movable furnishings, and remember that a visit to a reconstructed room of the period rarely gives a true impression of its appearance in the 16th or 17th century.

Some things, though, never change. The emotional importance of the fireplace in the Scottish domestic scene has remained unaltered for centuries. 'Hearth and home' is still a powerful sentiment, and many Scots today retain an open fire of logs or coal, or a stove, in addition to some form of central heating.

In renaissance Scotland permanent fires were required both for comfort and for cooking, and so the emotional and practical focus of the traditional home was to be found around the hearth or fireplace in Hall

Castle Restorations

**Specialists in restoring Interiors
of Castles, Stately Homes,
Ancient Monuments and
Buildings, Historic sites,
Town Houses etc . . .
Commisions accepted for Antique
reproduction furniture.
Restoration and repairs to
furniture expertly carried out**

**Auchtertool House
Auchtertool
Fife KY2 5XW
Tel: 0592 780371**

and kitchen. Indeed the chief room of the long house had been known to Norsemen as the 'fire house'. In Scottish tower houses this room has become known as the Great Hall and even in grand houses the Hall was the centre of life in the home — though rich families later chose to adopt more private quarters for their own use in the form of a solar or parlour, away from the communal life of the Hall.

The provision of a hearth is the most important factor in the consideration of early house plans, since the location of the fire directly affects the functioning of the house and how it was furnished. Architecture and furniture both serve the needs of the occupants, and the efficiency and comfort of a house are the outcome of generations of development. The concept of the house as a 'machine for living in' was not, after all, invented in the 20th century, though earlier generations might have phrased it differently!

To signal its import-ance in the life of the home, the fireplace was enriched to serve as the decorative focus of the room; and the Hall fireplace was usually the most elaborate of all.

Decorative plaster-work on stone vaults and overmantels is thought to be the work of journeyman plasterers who travelled widely and worked in Scotland and England in the early 17th century. In well-to-do homes, the chimney opening was provided with a carved fire surround, and surmounted with a stone, plaster or wooden over-mantel, often charged with the arms of the family and its associates. The heraldry above the fireplace in the Great Hall at Craigievar is one of the most magnificent examples of early plaster-work in Britain.

In addition to panelling and painting, the renaissance room was frequently hung with fabrics to keep out the winter draughts. Tapestries and embroidered cloth were also used for upholstery: long cushions to soften hard wooden benches and window seats, hangings, bedcovers and window covers. To the modern observer, the wooden-seated chairs and settles of the period represent cold comfort, but in fact most rooms were plentifully supplied with turkeywork, needlework or even plain cloth cushions. Fine carpets were used to cover tables and sideboards rather than floors.

Despite our increasing knowledge of furniture types we still have only a sketchy view of the predictable ways in which furniture was used in the early house. This is an important and relevant matter, since the design of individual pieces is often directly related to the exact use for which they were intended and the exact location for which they were made. A prime example is the usual form of the long dining table. Such a large piece of furniture was a cumbersome object in a house, so the layout of the Hall — which derived from the Norse longhouse — was designed expressly to accommodate the large table with its necessary seating.

Most houses, except the very poorest, contained a reasonable range of furniture types — a chair, a large table, a serving table, stools or backstools, chests for storage, a cupboard or

Gladstone's Land and Moubray House are surviving examples of merchants' houses in the Old Town of Edinburgh. Gladstone's Land is in the care of The National Trust for Scotland and furnished throughout with interesting and appropriate examples of renaissance interior style

two, beds — and the average inventory gives us a balanced view of the spread of furniture within the house.

Significantly, the table and chairs (or stools) are usually mentioned, as it were, in the same breath in inventory lists, and so we may assume that they were standing together when recorded. But occasionally we are lucky and the compiler may note ' . . . one oaken table and one oaken chair that standeth at the table's end . . .' (1594). Hundreds of wills and inventories refer to chests placed ' at the bed's feet', or 'at the stairshead', and these both represent common practice. The chest at the foot of the bed was especially useful for the safe storage of valuables during the night.

If the room was not panelled or painted, it might be hung with fabrics to keep out the draughts. The most desirable and effective draught-excluders were the thick woollen tapestries which were imported from Flanders, or later made in this country. Tapestry hangings were known by the generic name of 'arras', after the Flemish town which was famous for their manufacture, though other lighter materials were also in common use.

A much cheaper form of painted or stained cloths took the form of both room and bed hangings. These are common in British inventories though few examples survive today. They were generally made in imitation of tapestry, with a similar range of subjects, and were sometimes known as 'counterfeit arras'.

Decorated wallpapers were also in use throughout the 16th and 17th centuries, though it is very difficult to gauge just how common they were in Scotland. They are rarely mentioned, even in English inventories, since they were not movable goods; and being of an ephemeral nature very few traces of them remain. Sometimes scraps may be found under later papers or panelling, but most survivors are known because of their use as box and drawer linings.

In the later 17th century 'flock' papers were introduced from the Netherlands in which the design was printed first with glue. The paper was then dusted over with flock, the powdered and coloured ends of wool, which stuck to the glue and produced a pattern. Printed papers might also include two or more colours, and further details were sometimes added by stencil.

The subject matter of early paper hangings is highly varied. Some of the most popular were copies of fabric designs, especially silk damasks, and Samuel Pepys mentioned the 'counterfeit damask' paper used to hang the walls of his wife's closet. Pictorial subjects were very common, as were floral patterns based on contemporary needleworks. The papers were printed by hand from woodblocks about twelve inches or fourteen inches square, and those intended for wall hangings were made in lengths of twelve feet or so, to be stored and sold in rolls.

While there is slender evidence for the use of decorative colour in wall treatments — apart from painted ceilings and wall paintings — it seems fair to assume that the practise in the rest of Britain applied to Scottish houses too, given Scotland's strong links with France and Northern Europe.

Edited by kind permission of Victor Chinnery from his definitive publication, Oak Furniture: The British Tradition. *Antique Collectors' Club. 1979.*

3 4
Gibson Street, Glasgow
DESIGNWORKS
interior designers
& architects

A showroom for ideas
A professional design
service for all interiors,
large or small, domestic or
commercial.

041-339 9520

Tuesday - Saturday 10 am - 5 pm

Country Diary, National Trust and Parker Knoll Kitchens

Now available in Edinburgh

Exquisite, traditional British-made wooden kitchens which will give lasting satisfaction by virtue of their elegance, style and durable design. Choose from mahogany, pine and other tasteful finishes.

Exclusively available from:

Country Diary, National Trust and Parker Knoll Kitchens

44 Ratcliffe Terrace, Edinburgh. Telephone 031-662 4112

Elegance in Lighting and Fine Furnishing at

Dagné Day Limited

A superb collection of oriental porcelain, celadon, brass and gilt table lamps.
Handmade lampshades in fine silks, satin and chiffon.
Other items of ornamental porcelain and reproduction occasional furnishings also available.

33a MORNINGSIDE ROAD, EDINBURGH EH10 4DR
Telephone 031-447 3577
CLOSED ALL DAY WEDNESDAY

NATIONAL GALLERIES OF SCOTLAND

THE NATIONAL GALLERY

The Mound, Edinburgh

European painting from the 14th to the 19th Centuries, and Print Room.

NATIONAL GALLERY OF MODERN ART

Belford Road, Edinburgh

20th Century painting, sculpture and graphic art.

NATIONAL PORTRAIT GALLERY

Queen Street, Edinburgh

Scottish history through portraits; Print Room and reference section.

Open Monday to Saturday 10am-5pm; Sunday 2pm-5pm
For further information contact:
Department of Information,
National Galleries of Scotland,
The Mound, Edinburgh EH2 2EL
Telephone 031-556 8921

---

tielsa

Tielsa kitchens are out of this world. They add a new dimension to styling. To quality. To luxury. Each kitchen is hand-finished and individually crafted. All incorporating a host of innovative design features; and are available with advanced built-in appliances. Choose from a superb range and enjoy our superb service. We will design and plan your new kitchen—without obligation. And our skilled experts will provide professional installation. Discover a different world—in our showroom.

WD KITCHENS & BATHROOMS

Unit 17A, Elgin St. Industrial Estate, Dunfermline, Fife
Tel 0383-737100

Richly carved oak furniture, wallhangings and tapestries, maps and
prints, candlestands, tiles, a well-appointed hearth — these are some
ingredients of a renaissance interior . . .

*Blue and white ceramic flower vase doubles as a pot-pourri bowl and is shown here with
tulips, a favourite flower of the renaissance; crewel work fabrics, left and right:
embroidered floral and zigzag pattern. Vase, fabrics, tapestry and velvet cushions from
Remus. Crewel work cushion in Warner's 'Saranpur' multi-colour. 17th century map of
Islay by Blaeu, Kurdish rug covering blanket box*

. . . but their selection and placing needs judicious thought
to prevent the result from looking like a pastiche interior
set up for tourists. The interiors of the 16th and 17th
century looked fresh and full of colour, not, as is popularly
imagined, dark, stark and gloomy.

Living in Scottish renaissance interiors is the privilege
of a few. But an increasing number of Scots are becoming
interested in this period and its accoutrements, and for
them, the careful importation of selected objects — even
into a modern interior — can bring immense satisfaction.

There is something 'right' and 'timeless' in a simple
fireplace decorated with delftware tiles, an early map of
Scotland against white painted walls, a carved oak settle in a
flagstone hall, well-chosen tapestry cushions grouped on a
sofa, crewel-work curtains which are still made in pure
wool and cotton.

To capture the 'feel' of the age, a 17th century map of
Scotland seems a good place to start...

17th century maps of Scotland have the triple advantage of being decorative, informative and still within the financial reach of most houseowners. The most comprehensive series are those based mainly on the surveys undertaken by Timothy Pont, latterly minister of Dunnet in Caithness, in the 1590s. In the words of Robert Gordon of Straloch, who revised many of these surveys, Pont 'travelled on foot right through this kingdom, as no one before him had done; he visited all the islands, occupied for the most part by inhabitants hostile and uncivilised; being often stripped, as he told me, by the fierce robbers. But when, having returned, he prepared to publish the results of his labours, he was defeated by the greed of the printers and booksellers'.

It was only in 1654, many years after his death, that Pont's work was taken up by the greatest cartographical publisher of the age, Blaeu of Amsterdam, who published 46 maps of Scotland, covering every part of the country, in 1654. Practically all other regional maps of Scotland published during the course of the following century were based on this series.

Facsimile editions of many Blaeu maps are available, as is this reproduction of the general map of Scotland produced in 1652 by the great English cartographer, John Speed, which is published by the National Library of Scotland, and available from its bookshop.

Specialist outlets for original maps and facsimiles include Carson Clark and John Nelson.

Aberdeen Chairs cost a pretty penny these days, but Stuart Interiors reproduces a *cacqueteuse* with an interesting pedigree for rather less. The original of this American panel back armchair was made by a Scottish settler in New Jersey and is now on display at the American Museum, Bath.

Shapes is the largest Scottish stockist of oak reproduction furniture, which is growing in popularity all over Britain. At the extensive showroom you can see a range of four-poster beds, tables large enough for a Great Hall banquet, Jacobean style chairs and armchairs as well as handsome Knole sofas in soft hide upholstery, like the one illustrated, which is from the Ashley Workshops.

Stuart Interiors, in association with Tissunique Ltd., has recently developed a range of authentic renaissance fabrics in pure wool,

woven on Jacquard looms in Somerset by Renaissance Weavers. The Barrington Court Collection is available in Scotland through specialist interior decorators.

True to the spirit of Scottish Renaissance Interiors, upholsterer Fiona Macrae persuaded the monks of Fort Augustus Benedictine Abbey to allow her to photograph this backstool in appropriate surroundings. She re-covered the chair in 'Swans and Cygnets' a Renaissance Weavers fabric in 100% wool, copied from an original 16th century design.

Crewel work was popular for embroidered hangings to decorate beds and keep out draughts. It can be seen at Crathes and Gladstone's Land, and leading interior decorators stock samples. In 100% cotton embroidered in pure wool, it is typical of 17th century domestic embroidery which emulated brightly painted bedcover panels imported from India. The embroidered zigzag was popular too, called Hungarian point, flamestitch, Florentine or bargello work in tapestry.

Laura Ashley's 'Grape' pattern is copied from one of the most famous textiles of the late 17th century, the Bradford table carpet in the

Victoria and Albert Museum. Charles Hammond's 'Gaddesdon' is derived from a late 16th century crewel work design and available in linen or chintz to order through leading interior decorators throughout Scotland.

Blue and white tiles seem as fresh today as when they were imported into renaissance Scotland in great numbers through the east coast seaports. The town of Delft in Holland was a centre of production of tin-glazed tiles, many thousands of which were exported to decorate fire-surrounds, alcoves and skirtings. During the 17th century a tile making industry grew up in Britain to produce 'delftware'. Typical designs like those illustrated here can be found in antique shops as collectors' items. New tiles are available in Scotland from Denis Marsden-Williams or

R&S Robertson.
Where one bright idea
leads to another…
and another…

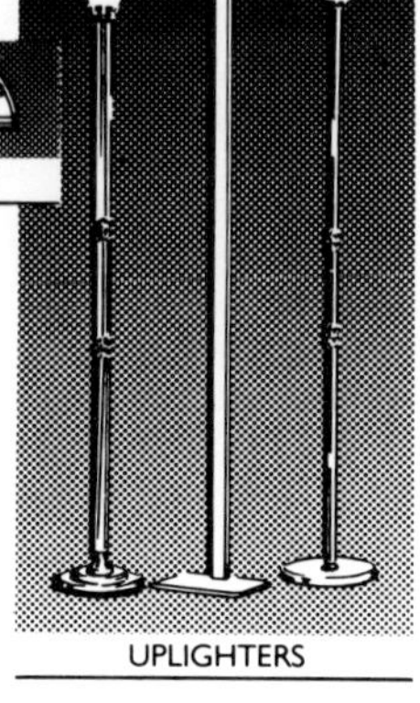

and another…

Look into our showrooms and
discover the best selection of lighting in Scotland.

OPEN 9 TO 5 TUESDAY-SATURDAY · 44 QUEEN STREET, EDINBURGH · TEL: 031-226 4750

Two Unique Mementos for Every Scot to Treasure

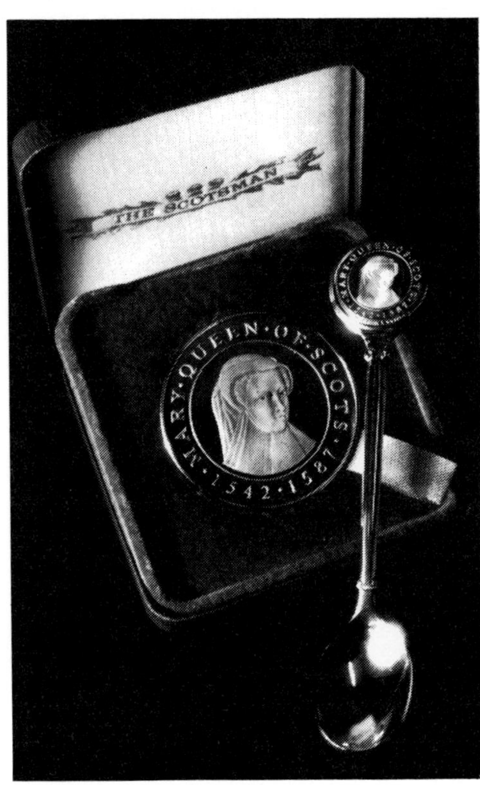

Commemorative Teaspoon
(inc postage & packing) Only **£2.00**

Solid Sterling Silver Medallion
(inc postage & packing) **£39.50**

To mark the historic 400th anniversary of the excecution of MARY QUEEN OF SCOTS at the hands of her royal cousin in England *THE SCOTSMAN*, in conjunction with the Tower Mint, proudly offers two superb mementos of a tempestuous life and a turbulent reign.

★ COMMEMORATIVE TEASPOON. This beautiful nickel-plated teaspoon with its ¾″ Golden Bronze Cameo Medallion is a special offer that will be prized by everyone … at a very special price

★ SILVER MEDALLION. This extremely handsome hall-marked Medallion is solid sterling silver (.925), is 1¾″ in diameter and 1oz troy weight. Mary Queen of Scots is depicted on one side and her seventh and last great seal on the reverse.

To take advantage of this special offer, please complete and return the coupon below, along with your cheque or postal order, or call in to our Front Office at 20 North Bridge.

To: Mary Queen of Scots Offers, Retail Unit, The Scotsman Publications Ltd, 20 North Bridge, Edinburgh EH1 1YT.

Please send me . . . . Commemorative Teaspoon/s*
and . . . . Medallion/s* (*insert or delete as applicable)

I enclose my cheque/postal order for £ . . . . made payable to The Scotsman Publications Ltd.

Name . . . .
Address . . . .
. . . . Post Code . . . .

Please allow up to 28 days delivery. Offer closes 30 Sept and applies to UK only. The Scotsman Publications Ltd, Regd Office, 20 North Bridge, Edinburgh EH1 1YT. Regd No 20911 Scotland.

through Stuart Interiors.

Domestic pottery and drinking pots were carted to many parts of Britain from Staffordshire. Slipware dishes (produced with trails of liquid clay called 'slip'), were widespread and popular in the 16th and 17th century. Jason Shackleton, the Scottish ceramicist, makes splendid 20th century equivalents like the photographed here.

Firelight and candle-light were vital to the lives of our ancestors — and continue to be valued for occasional use in many Scottish homes. Romantics and purists alike value well appointed fireplaces and a plentiful supply of candles and candle holders — sconces, candlestands, candlesticks. Jason Shackleton's ceramic candle-stand would look well in most interiors. Similar pieces can be seen at the Scottish Craft Centre.

Renaissance utensils were frequently of wood made by turners. Bowls, trenchers and goblets for tableware were almost completely supplanted by 19th century pottery. Pieces that have survived have a wonderful patina and are collectable as interesting and attractive objects. However, unpolished items are again being made for practical use both on the commercial market and by craftsmen.

Consult the Scottish Conservation Directory for furniture makers who might turn their talents to making a pricket candlestick or trencher to individual commission.

Pewter has been used in Britain since Roman times. Scottish pewter of the 16th and 17th century has become rare and vauable, avidly collected by owners of tower houses and admirers of the renaissance period. Stuart Interiors specialises in recreating typical 17th century pewter which is lead-free and entirely safe for everyday use.

Stuart Interiors is the leading British specialist firm in 16th and 17th century interior design. It offers a complete design and furnishing service for clients with early houses or for people who wish to recreate elements of traditional style. For example, Stuart Interiors is creating a renaissance interior within a Victorian lodge house in Aberdeenshire for a client who is hooked on the period. The firm's catalogue offers a comprehensive guide to the elements of renaissance interior style.

Renaissance tower houses boasted planned gardens laid out in formal designs. Some of the plants they used are still carefully cultured by specialist nurseries who stock varieties of old plants including herbs, roses, pinks, pansies and daisies. Plants from the Past specialises in pinks, and it is worth crossing the Border to Hetherton House Nursery to see the Physic Garden and the marvellous flower garden.

Carson Clark Gallery,
173 Canongate, Edinburgh
Tel: 031-556 4710

Castle Restorations,
Auchtertool House,
Auchtertool, Fife
Tel: (0592) 780371

Lennox Savage offers an interior design consultancy on early interiors and makes hand-dyed cotton hangings, cushions covers and other decorated fabrics to individual commissions. Her inspiration comes mainly from early sources. **Left to right:** *Books of Kells, Wild Rose, Medieval Whorl, Heraldic Motif. The design of the hangings on and behind the cacqueteuse chair is copied from the Aberlemno Stone of Angus, and the hanging in the window is based on a renaissance wallcarving.*

Charles Hammond Fabrics,
165 Sloane Street, London SW3
Tel: 01-235 2151

Conservation Bureau, SDA,
Rosebery House,
Haymarket Terrace, Edinburgh
Tel: 031-337 9525

Denis Marsden-Williams,
Coultknowe Farm, Dunning Glen,
Dollar
Tel: (0259) 81379

Fiona Macrae, Achnahannair,
Glen Lonan, Taynuilt, Argyll
Tel: (0320) 6377

Hetherton House Nursery,
Cambo, Northumberland
Tel: (067 074) 278

Jason Shackleton,
Lauriston Hall, Dumfries
Tel: (0387) 82472

John Nelson (Maps),
22 Victoria Street, Edinburgh
Tel: 031-225 4413

Laura Ashley,
137 George Street, Edinburgh
Tel: 031-225 1121

Laura Ashley,
215 Sauchiehall Street, Glasgow
Tel: 041-333 0850

Lennox Savage Interiors,
4a Howe Street, Edinburgh
Tel: 031-225 1781

London Interior Designers Centre,
2a Battersea Park Road,
London SW8 5BJ
Tel: 01-627 5000

National Library of Scotland,
George IV Bridge, Edinburgh
Tel: 031-226 4531

Plants from the Past,
Old Castle, Belhaven, Dunbar
Tel: (0368) 63223

Remus,
16 Stafford Street, Edinburgh
Tel: 031-225 6773

Renaissance Weavers,
Staple Court, Hockworthy,
Wellington, Somerset
Tel: (03986) 297

Scottish Craft Centre,
Acheson House,
140 Canongate, Edinburgh
Tel: 031-556 8136

Shapes,
33 West Mill Road, Colinton,
Edinburgh
Tel: 031-441 7963

Stuart Interiors,
Barrington Court, Barrington,
Ilminster, Somerset
Tel: (0460) 40349

In the Great Hall of Pitcullo in Fife the hearth still dominates a colourful interior. The fireplace is the original, but the beam-and-board ceiling was constructed recently by Castle Restorations, as were the shutters and doors. All the new woodwork is modelled on 17th century examples. The ceiling, one of a number in the house, was decorated by Michael Pinfold in a design based on local flowers and herbs. Crewel-work curtains, tapestry cushions, the sword above the fireplace, the painted door, carved furniture and studded shutters all evoke a 17th century atmosphere.

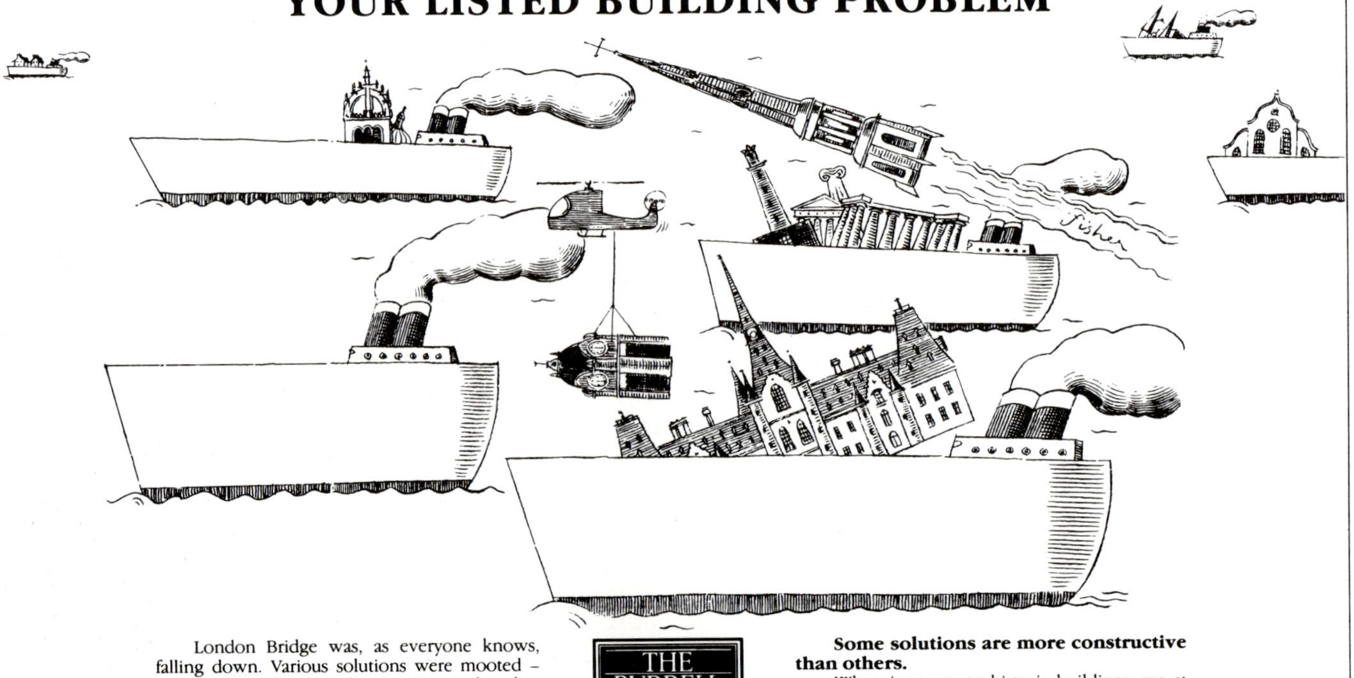

INSIDE INFORMATION

ANTIQUES · BOOKS · CLOCKS · CONSERVATORIES · FABRICS · FURNITURE INTERIOR DESIGN · METAL WORK · MUSICAL INSTRUMENTS · ORIENTAL RUGS · PAINTING & GILDING · WOODTURNING · STAINED GLASS · TEXTILES

J. & J. HARDIE ANTIQUES LTD

222/224 Newhaven Road
EDINBURGH, EH6 4JY

031-552 7080

RESTORATION OF 18TH AND 19TH CENTURY FURNITURE - TURNING, VENEERING, INLAYING, POLISHING, CARVING.

REPRODUCTIONS MADE TO SPECIAL COMMISSIONS

MURRAY-TAIT ANTIQUES AND FURNISHINGS, 51 MAYNE ROAD, ELGIN, MORAY IV30 1PF. Tel: (0343) 49313.
SUPPLIERS of quality furniture, antiques, fine fabrics, oriental artefacts. Cabinet making, upholstery and restoration service. Shipping services arranged. Please telephone for an appointment.

ELIZABETH LUMSDEN, BOOK-RESTORER, CRAFT BOOK-BINDER. SCOTSTOUN FARM, AMULREE, DUNKELD, PERTHSHIRE PH8 0EI. Tel: AMULREE 225.
Craft Bookbindings and Book Restorations undertaken. Repair and Conservation of Bindings in Calf, Sheep or Morrocco, Vellum and Cloth. Book Boxes and Slip Cases made.

J. CHRISTIE, BOOKBINDER
BINDING, REPAIRS & RESTORATION SERVICE TO MUSEUMS, LIBRARIES, LEGAL PRACTICES, INDIVIDUALS ETC. FULL MEMBER S.O.B.B.R.
UNIT 7, CANONGATE VENTURE,, NEW STREET, EDINBURGH 031-556 4073.

TOM VALENTINE - Bookbinding and Book Conservation, Unit 1, Dalderse Avenue, FALKIRK. Tel: (0324) 37049.
Specialists in book and document conservation. Complete libraries refurbished. Commissions for fine bindings undertaken.

CLOCKS: Simon Louman, MBHI Restoration and repair of fine clocks.
Cambier Clocks, Fowlers Hill, Dyce, Aberdeen. Tel: (0224) 722362.

Alan S. Hamshere,
CLOCK MAKER
**Balcanquhal Farmhouse, Gateside, Fife KY14 7SS.
Tel: (03376) 325.**
Specialists in the restoration and repair of antique clocks - turret clocks, stable clocks, musical clocks etc.
Makers of architectural clocks. Spring and weight driven clocks and musical and astronomical movements.
Restores dials, lacquer cases and gilding, wheel and pinion cutting, hands etc.

PENDULUM CLOCKS
Individually designed mechanical movements, case and dial in solid wood and brass, showing moving parts. Clients taste and traditional clockmakers skill create a unique timepiece to decorate any style of home.
J. TUBBECKE Clockmaker, 49 Island Street, GALASHIELS (0896) 56993.

Antique Clocks can be subject to alteration either to deceive or due to bad workmanship. Why not have an independent assessment of your clock's condition. Contact ROBERT BORTHWICK CMBHI, 73 WELLGATE, LANARK. Tel: (0555) 4887.

BROWN'S CLOCKS LTD. Established 1933 Fine Clocks and Watches Bought and Sold. Restoration and Repairs our Speciality
203 Bath Street, Glasgow G2 4BZ
Tel: 041-248 6760

CURTAIN BOUTIQUE, 46 MARIONVILLE ROAD, EDINBURGH, EH7 5UB. Tel: 031-661 8533.
Specialist curtain makers and soft furnishers. Curtains, blinds, bedspreads, loose covers expertly made and fitted. Extensive range of fabrics. Rails installed. Contract and Domestic enquiries invited.

Soft furnishings of all kinds

Chosen in your home – delivered to your home Tel: 041-952 9606
for a free and friendly quotation

SWAGS & TAILS
If you want to give your furniture a facelift or create that special new look for your home, our very personal service, our high quality upholstery and our intriguing range of curtain fabrics are just what you need.
7 Jeffrey Street, Edinburgh
Tel: 031-557 4480

RESTORATION & CONSERVATION OF ANTIQUE FURNITURE

WILLIAM R. TRIST
031-557 3828

Cabinet making, architectural mouldings, French polishing, cane & rush seating, chairmaking, turning.

9 CANONGATE VENTURE, NEW STREET, EDINBURGH.

Member of The Scottish Society for Conservation & Restoration

---

Douglas Weir
HOUSE FURNISHINGS

Specialists in Reproduction Furniture, Cabinet Making, French Polishing, Soft Furnishings.

347 Byres Road, Glasgow G12 8AR
Telephone 041-339 5673

193 Hyndland Road, Glasgow G12 9HT
Telephone 041-334 4514

WIL MARTIN BOWDEN SPRINGS FISHERY, LINLITHGOW 847269, FURNITURE MAKER AND RESTORER. **SPECIALIST IN CHARLES RENNIE MACKINTOSH REPRODUCTIONS.**

CLASSIC CONSERVATORIES

Classic Conservatories are architect designed, custom built, period style timber conservatories. Single or double glazed and always designed to blend with your home.
Free site visits and estimates in Central Scotland and Border areas.
Eskbank, Dalkeith, Midlothian   **Tel: 031-663 3173**

""

INSIDE INFORMATION

ANTIQUES · BOOKS · CLOCKS · CONSERVATORIES · FABRICS · FURNITURE · INTERIOR DESIGN · METAL WORK · MUSICAL INSTRUMENTS · ORIENTAL RUGS · PAINTING & GILDING · WOODTURNING · STAINED GLASS · TEXTILES